Legal Issues in the Music Industry

Legal Issues in the Music Industry

by

Mark J. Davis

Published by:

BuzzGig, LLC

PO Box 1533

Shreveport, LA 71165-1533

1st Edition: January 2010

Copyright © 2010 BuzzGig, LLC

All rights reserved

Printed in the United States of America

ISBN-10: 0-615-33686-8

ISBN-13: 978-0-615-33686-2

CONTENTS

INTRODUCTION

This work evolved out of lectures I have given in the Music Industry Studies Program at Loyola University of New Orleans since 2001. As an entertainment attorney who has specialized in copyright for 30 years & as a former arbitrator for the Copyright Office, I recognize that this topic is confusing and filled with misinformation, legalese, and old wives tales.

My goal is to provide a clear-cut approach to explaining why these complex legal issues lie at the foundation of the entertainment industry. Hundreds of students have benefited from this method, and I hope you will too.

Throughout the book, the symbol ⓘ indicates a URL where the reader can find more information on the topic.

Appendix A contains handouts, diagrams, sample contracts, and other explanatory material.

The symbol ◀ refers to a sound recording of the music discussed in the text. A full discography is contained in Appendix B.

MODULE 01: THE MUSIC BUSINESS

There are four roles in the music business: *Songwriter, Publisher, Recording Artist*, and *Record Label*. The relationship between the songwriter and Publisher is called the *Publishing side* of the business. The relationship between the Recording Artist and the Record Label is called the *Label side*.

It all begins with the Songwriter who composes a song. He owns the copyright because he created it himself. Copyright begins at the moment of creation – the moment an original expression of the songwriter is put in tangible form.

As you are taking notes, you are creating copyrighted material right now. As soon as the ink is dry on the paper, you hold the copyright to what you wrote. A podcast of this lecture holds a sound recording copyright. It is not on paper, but it is my voice on the tape. The expression of my ideas was put into fixed form on the tape. The sound recording, which is downloaded as an MP3 is the tangible form of my work.

SONGWRITER

The Songwriter is the one that creates the song. The term Songwriter includes composers and lyricists – they are partners in writing the composition. Songwriters have the copyright on the song they composed. They put their original thoughts into a fixed form. At that moment, the copyright begins. The Songwriter holds the copyright because he wrote the sheet music.

PUBLISHER

A *Music Publisher* turns a copyright into money. The Publisher enters into a contract with the Songwriter. The essence of the contract is as follows: *the Songwriter transfers the copyright to the Publisher. In exchange, the Publisher agrees to exploit the copyright and pay the Songwriter a percentage of all the money that the song earns.*

U.S. Copyright Act Section 106

Copyright is a bundle of rights as listed in Section 106 of the Copyright Act. In brief, they are:

- (1) The right to reproduce the work
- (2) The right to make derivatives
- (3) The right to distribute and sell the work
- (4) The right to perform the work in public.
- (5) The right to display the work in public.
- (6) For sound recordings only, the exclusive right to the digital audio transmission of the work

The concept of copyright not only applies to music, but it also to books, movies, sound recordings, plays, choreography, photographs, works of art, and sculpture; in short, all kinds of things. The rights granted in Section 106 are the ones that are exploited. These rights are how you make money from what you have created.

The basic concept embodied in the word ***copyright***, is the right to make a copy. Oddly enough, that is the one thing in law that is exactly what the jargon says it is, it is ***the right to make a copy***. Now if we move forward to §106(3), what is the point of having the right to make a copy if you cannot sell those copies? Reproduction, distribution, and sale are linked together. The copyright owner has the exclusive right to make copies, and the exclusive right to distribute and sell those copies. The copyright owner has the same power and right ***NOT to distribute the work***.

§106(2) is the right to prepare a derivative, meaning the copyright owner is the only one who can make changes to the original work. Any changes have to be authorized; otherwise, it is an infringement of the exclusive right to make a derivative.

For example, the copyright owner can change the ending of a movie, translate a song into another language, or publish a second edition of a book. The §106(2) derivative right allows the owner to edit, update, change the format of a work, and permit a movie to be made based on a novel.

Sections 106(4) and 106(5) are the rights to perform and display the work in public. Although this course approaches copyright from the music aspect, these rights apply to all copyrighted works. The right to perform and the right to display are twins. You cannot perform a piece of sculpture, however you can display a piece of sculpture. There is no money in displaying sheet music, just in its performance before an audience.

How To Make Money With Your Song

When a Songwriter creates a composition and enters into a contract with a Publisher, he transfers his copyright to the Publisher – which means he is *transferring ALL of the §106 rights*. After that written transfer (the publishing contract) is signed, the Publisher holds all the §106 rights. The Publisher is the only person that may authorize a derivative work. The Publisher alone grants the right to reproduce the work, or to distribute and sell it. The Publisher controls the performance and display of the work.

All of these §106 rights generate income and the Publisher has agreed to collect that income, to exploit that composition and split the money with the Songwriter. This is the essence of a publishing deal.

Copyright Is a Long Term Game

A Songwriter who composes a work today has the copyright until he dies, plus 70 years after his death. This means that his children, grandchildren, and great-grandchildren will inherit the copyright.

The secret of being rich in the music business is to write a hit song. Why? Because you are exploiting your §106 right to perform that composition and people are buying sheet music copies of that composition, and labels are reproducing the composition on a CD, distributing it, and selling it.

Publishing companies understand that having a hit composition in their *catalogue* (all the copyrights that it owns) will generate money every day until the copyright expires. It may be a small amount, but each and every day the copyright will generate income. People will be playing that hit song 20 years from now. It may be on the "Golden Oldies" radio station 40 years from now, but it will still be performed. That is the economic power of copyright – the ability to generate income over a very long period after the author has died.

THE LABEL SIDE

The other half of the business is generally called the *Label side*. The copyright that gets exploited on the publishing side of business is the letter C in the circle copyright: ©. A claim to ownership of a composition is registered on Form PA at the copyright office in Washington D.C. If you wrote a book, it would be Form TX. If you painted a picture or created a sculpture, or snapped a photo, Form VA would be appropriate for visual arts. There is another copyright form which only applies to sound recordings, Form SR. A registration on a sound recording copyright is indicated by the letter P in a circle: ℗.

Browse through your record collection and read the liner notes. On them, you'll see a listing of compositions written by various songwriters. The Publishers will be listed, with their performing rights organization affiliation (BMI, ASCAP, or SESAC). The symbol © with the year of creation will also be listed; for example:

"I Love You" composed by Aardvark & Zebra © 2010 XYZ Music Publishing Co. BMI

Those are the copyrights for the individual compositions. 10 songs on the album = 10 compositions = 10 copyrights. All 10 compositions are owned by various Publishers, and created by Songwriters.

On the back of the CD, you will find the copyright symbol for sound recordings, the letter P in a circle ℗ – with the name of the Record Label; for example:

℗ 2010 Sony Records

Note that there are two different copyrights in the music business. The same basic rights are exploited, not only under the Form PA copyright © for the compositions, but also under the Form SR copyright ℗ for the sound recordings of the performances of those compositions.

On the label side of the business, the Record Label usually owns the Form SR copyright ℗, that is, the §106 rights for the sound recording – not the underlying compositions that were performed on the record.

FOUR ROLES

The tricky thing about the record business is when we talk about these four roles: the Songwriter, the Music Publisher, the Recording Artist, and the Record Label; we can get easily confused. There are many cases where Songwriters are also Music Publishers. A Record Label might own a Publishing company. Recording Artists may also write their own songs, thus they are also Songwriters. Many Artists and Songwriters have their own Music Publishing companies or Record Labels.

Take the Beatles for example. They started as songwriters and signed a publishing deal. They realized after a while that they didn't like the publishing deal, and started their own publishing company. They were artists under contract to a label. After that contract ended, the Beatles started their own record label, Apple Records. This is an instance where Songwriters are also Publishers, Recording Artists, and owned a Record Label.

THE RECORDING ARTIST

The relationship between a Recording Artist and a Record Label is based on the exploitation of a sound recording. *The Artist is under contract to a Label to record his performance in exchange for a percentage of record sales.* That summarizes a 300-page recording contract in one phrase.

Of course a Recording Artist can make money in many other ways – live performances, by using their name on T-shirts and merchandise, or by endorsing a product. However, the exploitation of the sound recording is not the source of that income. Those are personal appearances, or the licensed use of an Artist's name and likeness for a T-shirt. Those are different rights that are being exploited, not copyright. Remember that *the Artist sells his recorded performance to the Label, not his live performance.* If he's playing live, he's getting the money, not the Label.

THE RECORD LABEL

The Record Label is the other end of the whole process. It's the most expensive end. What does it take to write a song? A pen and a piece of paper are very cheap. You can borrow a pen and you can borrow a piece of paper. Being a Publisher is really not that much more expensive. There are filing fees, Copyright Office fees, a telephone to call people who are licensing the songs, and a Rolodex for your desk. There is not a whole lot of capital investment necessary for a Publisher. Being a Recording Artist is inexpensive, just show up and play at the studio.

The Record Label pays for the entire production of the record, with no guarantee that anybody is going to buy it. The Label pays an advance to the Artist. The Label pays for the studio. The Label pays for the blank tape. The Label pays the engineer. The Label pays mixing and mastering costs. The Label pays money to Publishers. The Label pays to manufacture the CD. The Label pays for the graphics, artwork, and photos. The Label pays for packaging. The Label pays for the guys to load records on trucks and ship them to stores.

Maybe nobody's going to buy the record, if so; the Label loses its investment. That's the tough part about being a Record Label – there's no guarantee. People have to eat every day. People buy clothes every day. People don't have to buy records every day.

One thing we're going to discuss further in this course is how the old business model of manufacturing, pressing, and distributing records is rapidly changing. Labels know it and are searching for a different way to make money from the exploitation of the sound recording.

Section 106(6) provides the exclusive right of digital audio transmission for sound recordings only. This is an exclusive right just like the right to reproduce or distribute copies. Record Labels of the future will shift their income sources from selling actual copies of CDs to getting money from digital audio transmission, such as Internet downloads, podcasting, MP3s, webcasting, and satellite radio.

CONCLUSION

This is a simple overview about how the music business works – the four roles. If you're confused, and don't see how it all works ask yourself: "What rights are concerned? Is it a sound recording copyright ℗ or a Form PA copyright © for a composition? Is it on the Publishing side of the business or the Label side?"

Know the basic relationship: Songwriters and Publishers exploit the © copyright in the composition. The Recording Artist and Record Label exploit the ℗ copyright in the sound recording.

MODULE 02: HISTORY OF COPYRIGHT

THE URGE TO EXPRESS

The urge to create art as an expression is one of the hallmarks of Homo sapiens – the *thinking man*. Between 35,000 and 30,000 years ago, the Aurignacians of southern Germany created sophisticated art.

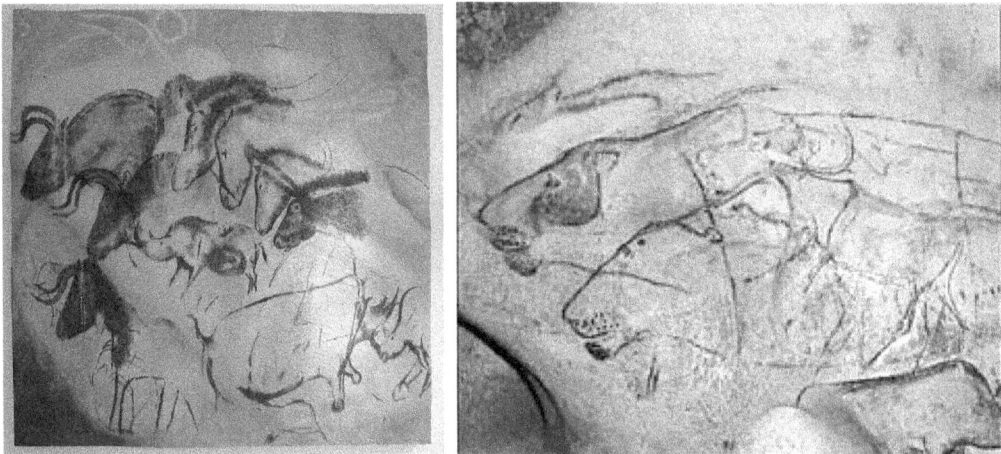

Drawing of Animals Chauvet-Pont-d'Arc

The Venus of Brassempouy, France

Oldest carving of the human form 27,000 B.C.E.

About 27,000 years ago, in the Cosquer caves, we find the painted outline of hands. Perhaps this was a ritual symbol, or perhaps the earliest claim to *Authorship*.

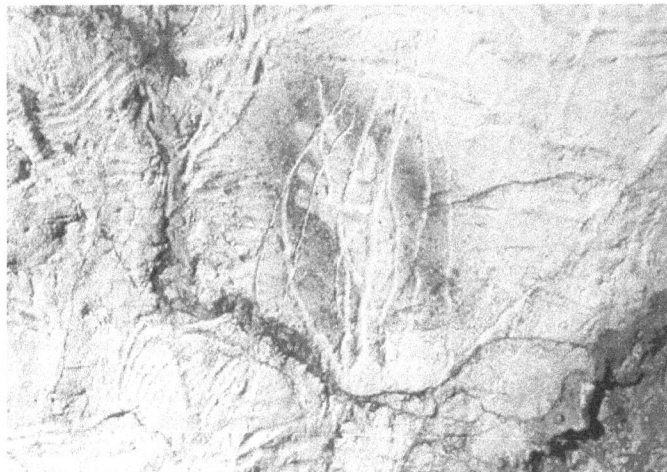

With the rise of Authorship, comes the free transmission of knowledge; at first through oral transmission of stories and later through the development of written language.

6,000 B.C.E.   Uruk clay tablets. Picture language evolves into written language

3,500 B.C.E.   The wheel is introduced in Sumeria

3,000 B.C.E.   Cuneiform tablets in Sumeria

2,600 B.C.E.	Earliest Egyptian poetry: *The Song of the Harper from the tomb of King Inyotef*: "Remember: it is not given to a man to take his goods with him. No one goes away and then comes back."
1,800 B.C.E.	Legal code of Hammurabi in Babylon
1,300 B.C.E.	The I Ching is written by Wen Wang, father of the Chou dynasty in China
1,250 B.C.E.	Genesis, first book of the Holy Bible: "...and God said let there be light: and there was light."
1,000 B.C.E.	Vedas and Upanishads composed in Sanskrit, holy texts of the Hindu religion: "Be subdued, Give, Be Merciful."
800 B.C.E.	Phoenician alphabet was invented
700 B.C.E.	Egyptian demotic script
700 B.C.E.	Homer wrote The Iliad and The Odyssey: "Sing Goddess of the wrath of Achilles, son of Peleus, who brought upon the Achaeans myriad woes and sent to Hades many a soul premature..."
550 B.C.E.	Lao Tzu wrote: "A journey of a thousand miles must begin with a single step."
500 B.C.E.	Confucius stated the Golden Rule: "What you do not want done to yourself, do not do to others."
450 B.C.E.	The *Old Testament* of the *Bible* is edited
441 B.C.E.	Sophocles writes *Antigone*
200 B.C.E.	*Old Testament* translated into Greek
100 A.D.	Paper invented in China

TRANSMISSION OF KNOWLEDGE

Technology's Limits

Since making copies was difficult and expensive, the author could easily control production and distribution of his work. The Romans and Greeks hired scribes to make copies of scrolls for sale. In Medieval Europe usually Church scribes were the only literate members of society. They had control of the ability to make copies and thus control of knowledge. The common folk got their news and current events from traveling troubadours who performed songs and told stories.

The Printing Press and Religion

In the 1450's Gutenberg invented the moveable type printing press, resulting in the widespread distribution of knowledge. It was arguably one of the most important inventions in history.

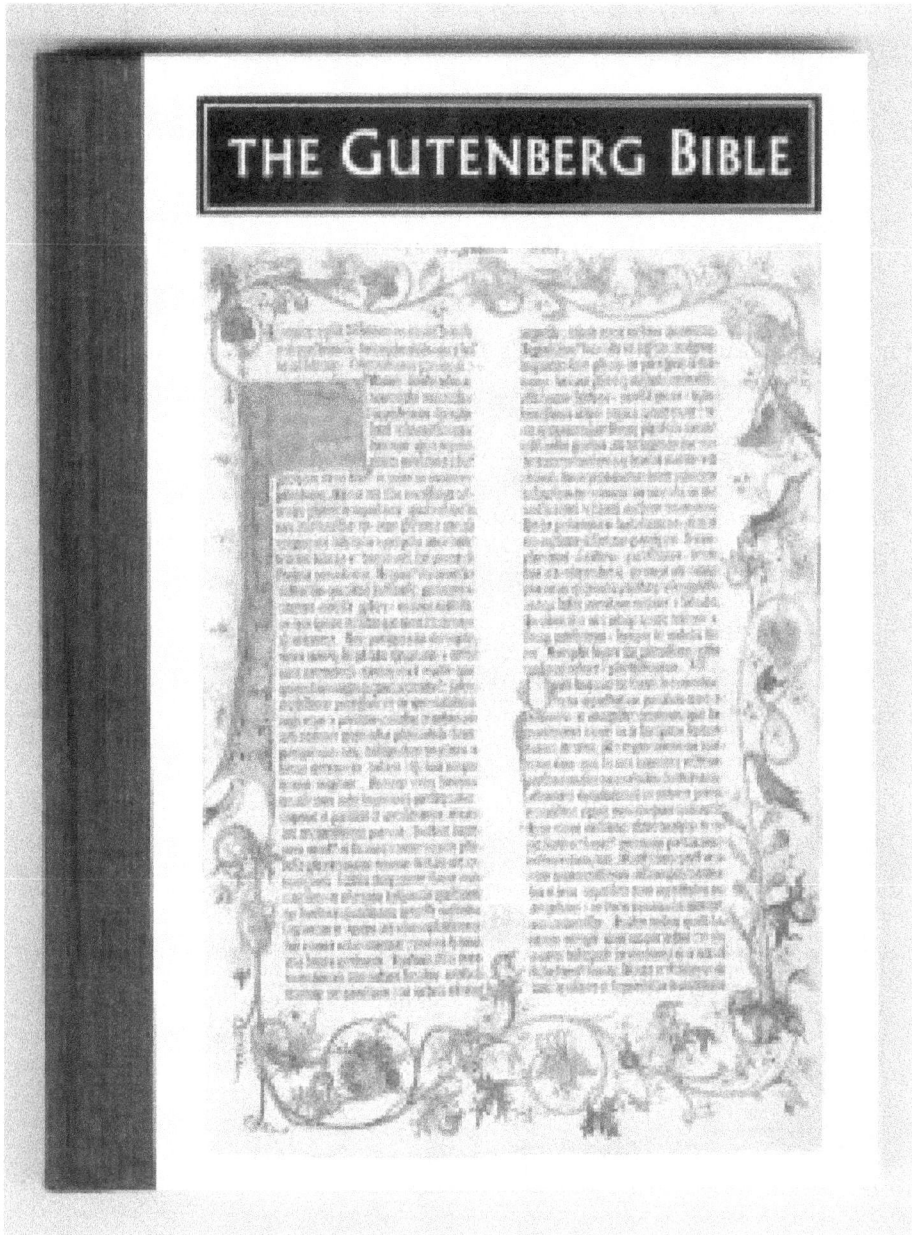

1455 Gutenberg Bible published in Mainz

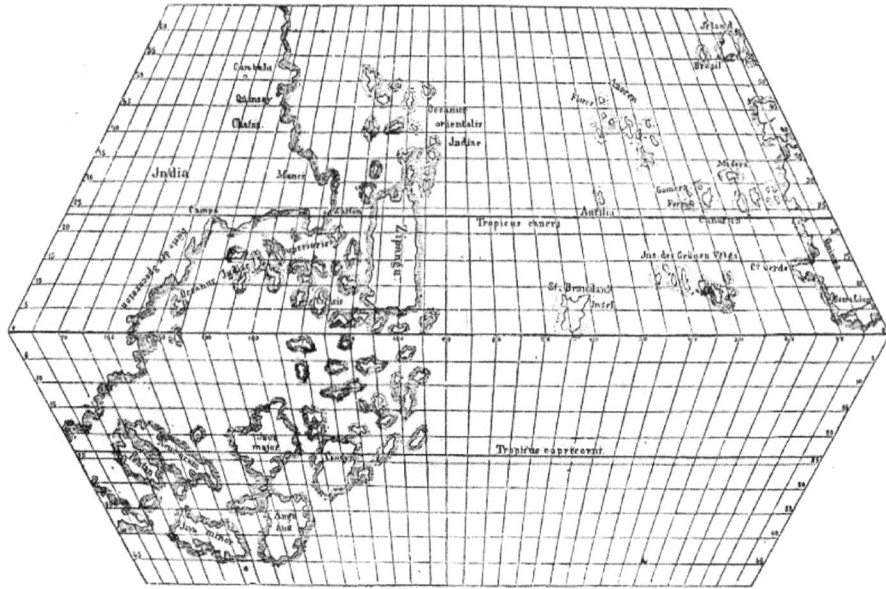

Christopher Columbus used Toscanelli's 1474 Map of the World on his voyage to the New World

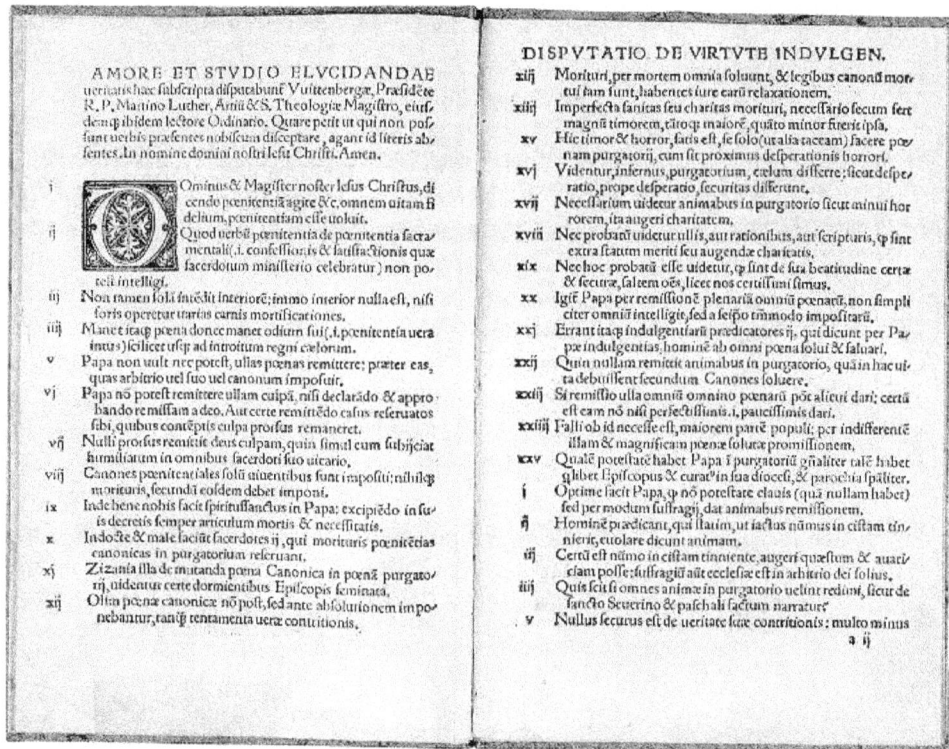

On October 31, 1517 Martin Luther's *Disputation on the Power and Efficacy of Indulgences* commonly known as *The 95 Theses* triggered the Protestant Reformation.

> **Thesis 27**
> They preach only human doctrines who say that as soon as the money clinks into the money chest, the soul flies out of purgatory.
>
> **Thesis 66**
> The treasures of indulgences are nets with which one now fishes for the wealth of men.
>
> **Thesis 86**
> Why does not the Pope, whose wealth is today greater than the wealth of the richest Croesus, build this one basilica of St. Peter with his own money rather than with the money of poor believers?

1522 Martin Luther translated the Bible from Latin into German

1532 Machiavelli's *The Prince* published

1534 Jesuit Order founded by St. Ignatius Loyola

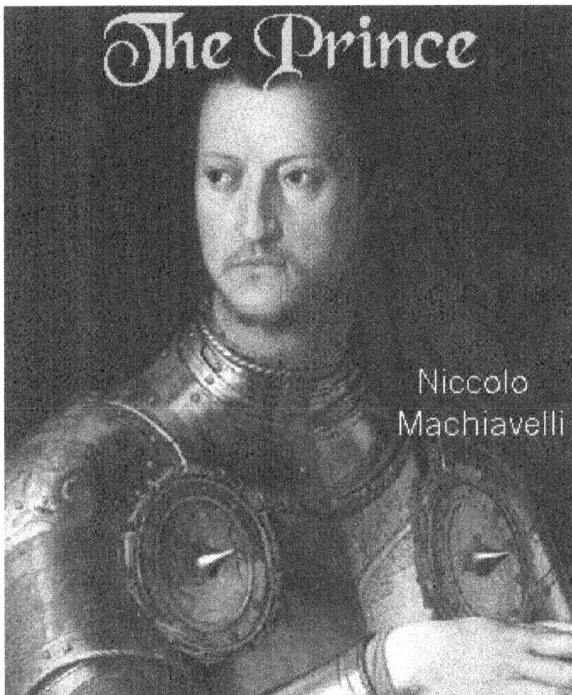

"Men ought either to be well treated or crushed…

Injury ought to be of such a kind

that one does not fear revenge."

S. IGNATIVS LOYOLA AVTHOR, FVNDATOR, ET PRIMVS

"To give and not to count the cost;

To fight and not to heed the wounds;

To toil and not to seek for rest…"

LEGAL LIMITS ON COPYING

Royal Monopolies

The first legal protections were granted by kings to favored authors and artists on a case-by-case basis. Albrecht Dürer, the German woodcut engraver had one of the clearest copyright warnings ever in 1511:

> Hold! You crafty ones, strangers to work, and pilferers of other men's brains. Think not rashly to lay your thievish hands upon my works. Beware! Know you not that I have a grant from the most glorious Emperor Maximillian, that not one throughout the Imperial Dominion shall be allowed to print or sell fictitious imitations of these engravings? Listen! And bear in mind that if you do so, through spite or through covetousness, not only will your goods be confiscated, but your bodies also placed in mortal danger.

1534 Licensing Act of England

The development of the printing press made it possible to make multiple copies quickly and cheaply. Literary works flourished, as did works of political and religious dissent. King Henry VIII's concern about political dissent led to the requirement that a publisher must first obtain a license before printing. Since the Crown could grant or withhold permission to print, it created a monopoly over the reproduction of a work. It also effectively served as censorship. Unapproved books were not printed.

1535 King Henry VIII broke with the Pope and established the Church of England.

1543 Copernicus printed *On The Revolutions of the Celestial Spheres*, and argued that the Earth was not the center of the solar system.

1559 Pope Paul IV responded to the flood of new ideas by censoring authors by listing their works in the *Index of Forbidden Books*.

1557 Stationers' Company

Queen Mary granted the Stationers' Company a monopoly over publication of all books in England. They registered which printer had the license to print a book, the *"copy-right"* and also held the power to destroy illegal copies. The right to control the physical copies themselves was granted to the printer, not the author.

1565 The pencil invented by Gessner.

1575 English music printing monopoly granted to composers William Byrd and Thomas Tallis (chief composer for the new Church of England).

1611 King James Bible published in English

1623 Publication of Shakespeare's First Folio

1694 Licensing Act expired after 160 years which led to increased competition between publishers

1704 First lending library in Berlin

1710 Statute of Anne – the Origin of Modern Copyright Law

Its full title, "An Act for the Encouragement of Learning, by vesting the Copies of Printed Books in the Authors or purchasers of such Copies, during the Times therein mentioned" is echoed in the U.S. Constitution.

The fundamental protections granted to authors embodied in this law are still used today:

- Encouraging learned men to write
- Requiring the consent of authors or assignees to make copies
- Limited time of protection (14 years from 1st publication)
- Granting a second term of 14 years (if the author was still alive)
- Providing for the seizure and destruction of infringing copies
- Allowing authors to sue infringers
- Public Domain after expiration of protection

Cup 19

Anno Octavo

Annæ Reginæ.

An Act for the Encouragement of Learning, by Veſt-
ing the Copies of Printed Books in the Authors or
Purchaſers of ſuch Copies, during the Times therein
mentioned.

Whereas Printers, Bookſellers, and other
Perſons have of late frequently taken
the Liberty of Printing, Reprinting,
and Publiſhing, or cauſing to be Printed, Reprinted, and Publiſhed Books,
and other Writings, without the Conſent of the Authors or Proprietors of
ſuch Books and Writings, to their
very great Detriment, and too often
to the Ruin of them and their Fami-
lies : For Preventing therefore ſuch
Practices for the future, and for the
Encouragement of Learned Men to Compoſe and Write uſe-
ful Books ; May it pleaſe Your Majeſty, that it may be Enacted, and be it Enacted by the Queens moſt Excellent Majeſty,
by and with the Advice and Conſent of the Lords Spiritual and
Temporal, and Commons in this preſent Parliament Aſſembled,
and by the Authority of the ſame, That from and after the
Tenth Day of April, One thouſand ſeven hundred and ten, the
Author of any Book or Books already Printed, who hath not
Transferred to any other the Copy or Copies of ſuch Book or
Books, Share or Shares thereof, or the Bookſeller or Bookſellers, Printer or Printers, or other Perſon or Perſons, who
hath or have Purchaſed or Acquired the Copy or Copies of any
Book or Books, in order to Print or Reprint the ſame, ſhall
have the ſole Right and Liberty of Printing ſuch Book and
Books for the Term of One and twenty Years, to Commence
from the ſaid Tenth Day of April, and no longer ; and that
the Author of any Book or Books already Compoſed and not
Printed and Publiſhed, or that ſhall hereafter be Compoſed, and
his Aſſignee, or Aſſigns, ſhall have the ſole Liberty of Printing
and Reprinting ſuch Book and Books for the Term of Four-

. 6   Ttt 2   teen

The Statute of Queen Anne

The Age of Enlightenment sparked political upheaval, the end of divine right of kings, and the birth of the United States. The rise of capitalism fed the free transmission of ideas which changed the world.

1716 First daily newspaper *Il Diario de Roma* published by Luca and Giovanni Cracas.

1768-1771 *Encyclopedia Britannica* published in Edinburgh by Adam and Charles Black.

Political Revolution

Thomas Paine wrote *Common Sense*, and it was released on January 10, 1776. When the population of the 13 Colonies was roughly 2 million people, *Common Sense* sold over 120,000 copies – one out of every sixteen Colonists bought this 46 page pamphlet.

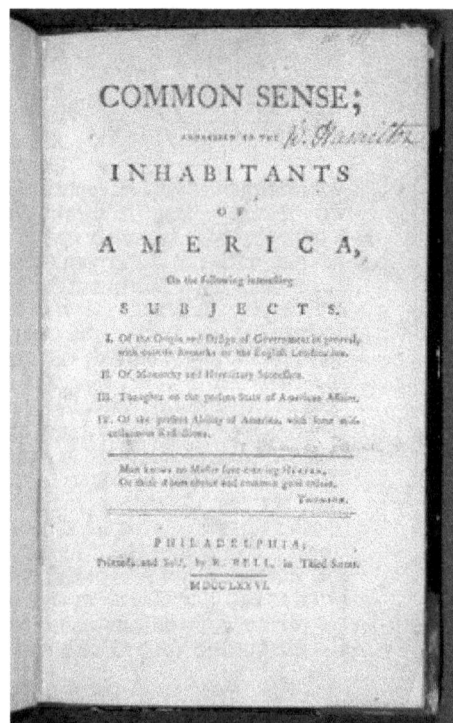

"The cause of America is in a great measure the cause of all mankind."
Portrait of Thomas Paine and Alexander Hamilton's copy of Common Sense

July 4, 1776 Declaration of Independence

1781 ARTICLES OF CONFEDERATION

The first copyright law in America was passed by the Connecticut Legislature in 1783. Noah Webster traveled to all 13 states seeking protection for his *American Spelling Book*.

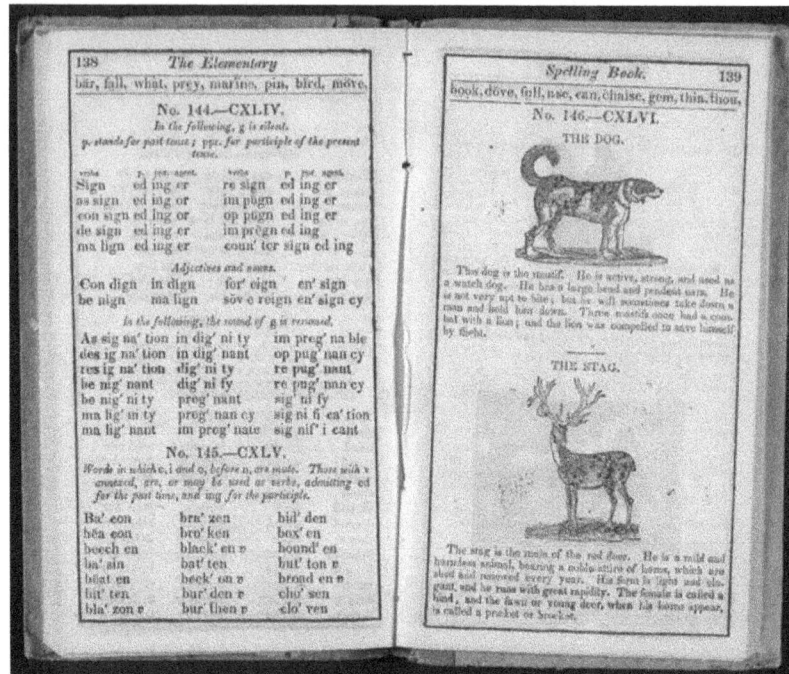

Eventually twelve states (all but Delaware) had copyright statutes. Protection differed from state to state. It was burdensome for an author to register his work in all states. When the Constitutional Convention met to amend the Articles of Confederation, they addressed the need for a uniform system of copyright. The Framers of the Constitution sympathized with authors and understood the value of a nation-wide system of copyright for the country.

1789 U.S. CONSTITUTION

The Founding Fathers were authors in their own right and well read men:

Thomas Jefferson, Founder of University of Virginia

Patrick Henry, author, orator, and Governor of Virginia

John Adams, attorney and author

Ben Franklin, author, printer and publisher *Poor Richard's Almanac*

Henry Knox, bookseller, first Secretary of War

James Madison, graduate of Princeton, chief author of the Constitution

They understood the importance of a mechanism to encourage writers and protect their works. This philosophy led directly to the constitutional provision on copyright. It is also the basis for U.S. patent law.

> **United States Constitution, Article I, Section 8**
>
> The Congress shall have Power…To promote the Progress of Science and useful Arts, by securing for limited Times to Authors and Inventors the exclusive Right to their respective Writings and Discoveries.

The language in the Constitution can be clearly traced back to the Statute of Anne whose full title was "An Act for the Encouragement of Learning, by vesting the Copies of Printed Books in the Authors or Purchasers of such Copies, during the Times therein mentioned."

Debates over the ratification of the Constitution took place in all the States. In New York, James Madison (later the 4th President), Alexander Hamilton (Washington's Secretary of the Treasury) and John Jay (later Chief Justice of the Supreme Court) wrote *The Federalist Papers*. It was a series of anonymous newspaper articles addressed to "The People of the State of New York", which explained the benefits of the proposed Constitution.

James Madison   Alexander Hamilton   John Jay

1790 COPYRIGHT ACT

Although the Constitution gave Congress the power to grant copyrights and patents to "Authors and Inventors", there was no mechanism for doing so. Authors applied to Congress for private bills establishing their rights. On May 31, 1790, President George Washington signed the first U.S. Copyright Act into law.

The Copyright Act of 1790 made the Federalist's arguments for protection of authors a part of the law.

- Copyright only for books, maps, and charts
- Limited time of protection (14 years from date of registration)
- Granted a second term of 14 years (if the author was still alive)
- Copyright notice and deposit required

Columbian Centinel.

Printed and published, on WEDNESDAYS and SATURDAYS, by BENJAMIN RUSSELL, in *State-Street*, BOSTON, MASSACHUSETTS.

Whole No. 660] *SATURDAY*, JULY 17, 1790. [No. 36—*of* VOL. XIII.

LAWS of the UNITED STATES.
PUBLISHED

By Authority.

CONGRESS *of the* UNITED STATES:
AT THE SECOND SESSION,
Begun and held at the City of New-York, on Monday the 4th of January, 1790.

An ACT for the ENCOURAGEMENT of LEARNING, by securing the Copies of Maps, Charts and Books, to the Authors and Proprietors of such Copies, during the Times therein mentioned.

BE *it enacted by the* SENATE *and* HOUSE *of* REPRESENTATIVES *of the United States of America, in Congress assembled*, That from and after the passing of this act, the author and authors of any map, chart, book or books already printed within these United States, being a citizen or citizens thereof, or resident within the same, his or their executors, administrators or assigns, who hath or have not transferred to any other person the copy-right of such map, chart, book or books, share or shares thereof; and any other person or persons, being a citizen or citizens of these United States, or residents therein, his or their executors, administrators or assigns, who hath or have purchased or legally acquired the copy-right of any such map, chart, book or books, in order to print, reprint, publish or vend the same, shall have the sole right and liberty of printing, reprinting, publishing and vending such map, chart, book or books, for the term of fourteen years from the recording the title thereof in the Clerk's Office, as is herein after directed: And that the author and authors, of any map, chart, book or books already made and composed, and not printed or published, or that shall hereafter be made and composed, being a citizen or citizens of these United States, or resident therein, and his or their executors, administrators or assigns, shall have the sole right and liberty of printing, reprinting, publishing and vending such map, chart, book or books, for the like term of fourteen years from the time of recording the title thereof in the Clerk's office as aforesaid: And if, at the expiration of the said term, the author or authors, or any of them, be living, and a citizen or citizens of these United States, or resident therein, the same exclusive right be continued to him or them, his or their executors, administrators or assigns, for the further term of fourteen years: *Provided*, he or they shall cause the title thereof to be a second time recorded and published in the same manner as is herein after directed, and that within six months before the expiration of the first term of fourteen years aforesaid.

And be it further enacted, That if any other person or persons from and after the recording the title of any map, chart, book or books, and publishing the same as aforesaid, and within the times limited and granted by this Act, shall print, reprint, publish or import, or cause to be printed, reprinted, published or imported, from any foreign kingdom or state, any copy or copies of such map, chart, book or books, without the consent of the author or proprietor thereof, first had and obtained in writing, signed in the presence of two or more credible witnesses; or knowing the same to be so printed, reprinted or imported, shall publish, sell, or expose to sale, or cause to be published, sold, or exposed to sale, any copy of such map, chart, book or books, without such consent first had and obtained in writing as aforesaid, then such offender or offenders shall forfeit all and every copy and copies of such map, chart, book or books, and all and every sheet and sheets, being part of the same, or either of them, to the author or proprietor of such map, chart, book or books, who shall forthwith destroy the same: And every such offender and offenders shall also forfeit and pay the sum of fifty cents for every sheet which shall be found in his or her possession, either printed or printing, published, imported or exposed to sale, contrary to the true intent and meaning of this Act, the one moiety thereof to the author or proprietor of such map, chart, book or books, who shall sue for the same, and the other moiety thereof to and for the use of the United States, to be recovered by action of debt in any court of record in the United States, wherein the same is cognizable: *Provided always*, That such action be commenced within one year after the cause of action shall arise, and not afterwards.

And be it further enacted, That no person shall be entitled to the benefit of this Act, in cases where any map, chart, book or books, hath or have been already printed and published, unless he shall first deposit, and in all other cases, unless he shall before publication deposit a printed copy of the title of such map, chart, book or books, in the Clerk's office of the district court where the author or proprietor shall reside: And the clerk of such court is hereby directed and required to record the same forthwith, in a book to be kept by him for that purpose, in the words following, (giving a copy thereof to the said author or proprietor, under the seal of the court, if he shall require the same) "District of to wit: *Be it remembered*, That on the day of in the year of the independence of the United States of America, A. B. of the said district, hath deposited in this office the title of a map, chart, book or books, (as the case may be) the right whereof he claims as author or proprietor, (as the case may be) in the words following, to wit: [here insert the title] in conformity to the act of the Congress of the United States, intituled, "An act for the encouragement of learning, by securing the copies of maps, charts and books to the authors and proprietors of such copies, during the times therein mentioned. C. D. Clerk of the District of ". For which the said clerk shall be entitled to receive sixty cents from the said author or proprietor, and sixty cents for every copy under seal actually given to such author or proprietor as aforesaid. And such author or proprietor shall, within two months from the date thereof, cause a copy of the said record to be published in one or more of the newspapers printed in the United States, for the space of four weeks.

And be it further enacted, That the author or proprietor of any such map, chart, book or books, shall, within six months after the publishing thereof, deliver, or cause to be delivered to the Secretary of State a copy of the same, to be preserved in his office.

And be it further enacted, That nothing in this Act shall be construed to extend to prohibit the importation or vending, reprinting or publishing within the United States, of any map, chart, book or books, written, printed or published by any person not a citizen of the United States, in foreign parts or places without the jurisdiction of the United States.

And be it further enacted, That any person or persons who shall print or publish any manuscript, without the consent and approbation of the author or proprietor thereof, first had and obtained as aforesaid, (if such author or proprietor be a citizen of or resident in these United States) shall be liable to suffer and pay to the said author or proprietor all damages occasioned by such injury, to be recovered by a special action on the case founded upon this Act, in any court having cognizance thereof.

And be it further enacted, That if any person or persons shall be sued or prosecuted for any matter, act or thing done under or by virtue of this Act, he or they may plead the general issue and give the special matter in evidence.

FREDERICK AUGUSTUS MUHLENBERG,
Speaker of the House of Representatives.
JOHN ADAMS, *Vice President of the United States, and President of the Senate.*
Approved, May the 31st, 1790.

George Washington,
President of the United States.
(True copy) THOMAS JEFFERSON,
Secretary of State.

☞ *The* ACT, *intitled*, "An Act for finally adjusting and satisfying the claims of Frederick Wm. de Steuben"—*An Act intitled*, "An Act for giving effect to an Act, intitled, "an Act to establish the Judicial Courts of the United States," within the State of North-Carolina"—*and an Act, intitled*, "an Act supplemental to the Act for establishing the salaries of the Executive Officers of Government, with their Assistants and Clerks"—*were inserted in* THE CENTINEL *of June* 10, 1790. *According to their dates, they follow the above.*

MISCELLANY.

OBSERVATIONS on the MANUFACTURES and COMMERCE of the United States.
By *W. BARTON*, of *Philadelphia.*
(CONTINUED FROM OUR LAST).

PAPER-HANGINGS, equal in quality and cheapness to any imported, are manufactured in large quantities by Mr. William Poyntell, and Messrs. Le Collay and Chardon, at Philadelphia; by Messrs. Mackay and Dixey, at Springfield, in New-Jersey; and other places in the Union*.

A great progress has been made in the manufacture of hosiery, in this country; and, with proper encouragement, much more may be accomplished in that branch. Mr. Burnaby, (in his travels through the middle settlements of North-America, in the years 1759 and 1760) notices the high estimation in which the Germantown stockings were then held; and this gentleman mentions his having been credibly informed, that two years before that period, there were manufactured, in that town, sixty thousand dozen pair; the common retail price of which was a dollar per pair. This, however, is conceived to be a mistake—it is probable that six thousand dozen pair was meant, as a redundant cypher (perhaps an errour of the press) makes this difference. Admitting this to be the case—and supposing that stockings of such a quality, manufactured abroad, would have cost the importer six shillings and three pence, or five-sixths of a dollar per pair; the actual saving to the country, by that number, amounted to 60,000 dollars. Besides this, a number of valuable citizens were supported by the manufacture, and the raw materials were supplied from our own farms. The writer of this paper does not know what quantity of hosiery is annually made at Germantown: But great improvements are daily making there in this manufacture—worsted, cotton, and thread stockings of an excellent quality and fabrick, may be purchased at that place (and twice a week at the market-house in this city) at very reasonable prices.

Wool and cotton cards, of American manufacture, now wholly supply the consumption of the country—they are not only superiour in quality to the British but † cheaper. The principal manufactures of this article are Messrs. Westcott and Adgate, of Philadelphia; and Messrs. Giles Richards and Co. of Boston.

Our farmers are directing their attention to dairies: And we are now furnished with large supplies of excellent American cheese.

The establishment of ‡ glass-houses would prove so beneficial to the undertakers, in many situations within the United States—that a very few years will probably place them among our most considerable manufactories.

NOTES.

* *We wish the inquiries of the respectable writer of these observations had been further extended—as a number of manufactories are carried on largely in the New-England States, which he has not mentioned—In particular, Paper-Hangings were printed in this town, before they were in any other on the continent—and we have now several respectable manufactories of these articles at work, viz. Messrs. Prentiss and May's, Mr. Hovey's, and Mr. Grant's.* CENT.

† *Wool cards have been exported from this country to Great Britain: And our Manufactures of this article have undersold the English in their own country.*

‡ *Prior to the year 1746, Ireland imported glass from other countries. At length, the Irish began to make some progress in this manufacture; and, in 1781, they first began to export glass.*

The great and increasing consumption of window-glass and bottles, in this country, should operate as a powerful motive for encouraging the glass-manufactories already established in some of these states, and for promoting the speedy establishment of similar works in other parts of the Union.—The glass manufactory on the Patowmack, it is said, gives employment to five hundred persons.

The printing of calicoes, cottons, and linens, may be expected to increase in proportion as we extend the manufactures of those articles: And the muslins and white calicoes imported from India, will likewise give employment to our calico printers. Mr. John Hewson, and Mr. Robert Taylor, both in the neighbourhood of this city, are masterly workmen in this branch: The former obtained a premium from the manufacturing society for the best specimens of printed goods.

In the state of Pennsylvania, there are twenty-one powder mills, capable of making six hundred and twenty-five tons of powder, per annum. This is retailed at five dollars per quarter, of 25lbs; and is offered for sale in larger quantities under sixteen dollars per cwt. The English price, after deducting the bounty of 4/6, is 75/6 sterling; or, about sixteen dollars and seventy-eight cents, per cwt. Independently of the importance of this article, as a means of national defence, the manufacture of it in this state is worth two hundred thousand dollars per annum. It is said, that the largest gunpowder works existing any where, are those at Frankford, near Philadelphia—now the property of Mr. Joseph J. Miller. The mill-work is constructed on the model of Mr. Rumsey's improvement of Barker's mill; Mr. Miller having purchased a licence from the patentee.

So much is done by the sugar refineries at Philadelphia, that although the medium of the annual import of brown sugar, into this port, is 5,692,848lbs. the amount of loaf sugar imported here is only 4,480lbs.* This business is also carried on at other places in the Union.

The annual amount of molasses, imported at Philadelphia, averages about 543,000 gallons; a great proportion of which is converted into spirits, in our distilleries: But, in the eastern states, this manufactory is much more extensive; insomuch that † the New-England rum is a considerable article of the American commerce. It is not to be expected, that the use of ardent spirits will ever be entirely dispensed with; and, therefore, we may wish success to our distilleries.

The culture and manufacture of silk are yet in their infancy, with us. In Connecticut indeed, this valuable article has obtained a respectable footing; through the skill and preserverance of Mr. Nathaniel Aspinwall (who may be truly stiled the promoter of the silk culture in that state) and under the patronage of the venerable and publick spirited Dr. Stiles. The writer of this article has observed, with pleasure, the laudable endeavours of Mr. Aspinwall, to promote the culture of silk in Pennsylvania and New Jersey; this indefatigable person has propagated many thousand of the Italian white mulberry-tree, in the vicinity of this city: And there is good reason to expect, that, in a few years hence, the citizens, of this state will deceive ample profit from their labours. The mulberry-tree, independently of its furnishing the best food for the silk worms—is a valuable timber for

NOTES.

* *From the 18th of March 1784, to the 17th of March 1785, there were imported to Philadelphia 1,406,000 lbs. of brown sugar, and 38 75lbs. of loaf sugar. Of the former, were exported 667,687lbs; and, of the latter, 19,800lbs. The imports of brown sugar to Philadelphia, from the 1st of November 1786, to the 31st of October 1787 (inclusive) amounted to 5,616,000lbs.; and of loaf sugar, but 2,362lbs. 434 762lbs. of the brown sugar were exported. In the year 1787, 63,752lbs. of loaf sugar were exported from the port of Boston. The progress that is making in the manufacture of Maple sugar, will greatly lessen the demand for foreign sugar.*

† *The New England rum exported from Boston, in the year 1787, is estimated at* [illegible]

The Copyright Act of 1790

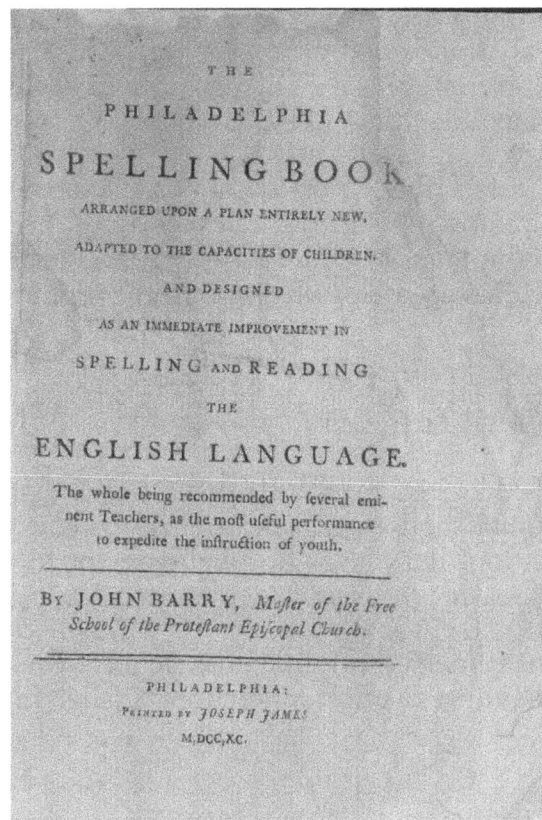

The Philadelphia Spelling Book by John Barry

The first work protected by U.S. copyright, June 9, 1790

A PROPERTY IN RIGHTS

James Madison is considered one of the greatest political thinkers of his time and the father of U.S. Copyright. He articulated a simple, yet novel idea – first published in *The National Gazette* in 1792, which is carved on the walls of the Copyright Office.

> AS A MAN IS SAID TO HAVE A RIGHT TO HIS PROPERTY;
>
> HE MAY BE EQUALLY SAID
>
> TO HAVE A PROPERTY IN HIS RIGHTS.

The owner of a thing can use it, enjoy what it produces, or destroy it as he wishes. In Roman Law, these 3 rights are called: *Usus, Fructus, and Abusus.* For example, a tree can provide lumber, bear fruit or be burned for warmth. Madison made an intellectual leap. If an owner could exercise these rights in a physical thing, he could also exercise the same rights in an intangible thing, like copyright.

Extending the concept further, if an owner of a piece of tangible property could lease out its use, yet retain ownership; so can a copyright owner license the use of his work, yet retain ownership. This is the heart of the entertainment industry; earning money from use of the rights granted under copyright protection of music and books.

REVISIONS OF COPYRIGHT LAW

The Act was amended in 1802 to include protection for prints. A notice of copyright was required on each published copy. The exclusive right to make derivative works was also implied by stating that it was an infringement to sell a print created by *"by varying, adding to, or diminishing the main design"* of another print.

An 1819 amendment conferred original jurisdiction over copyright in federal courts only, and gave them the power to grant injunctions against infringers.

1831 General Revision

- Important changes were made in the first of four major revisions of the 1790 Act:
- Musical compositions were protected (but not their public performance)
- 28 year original term of copyright
- 14 year renewal right given to the author or his widow
- Copyright notice requirements were simplified
- No protection if the work was published without a copyright notice

19th Century Amendments

A dozen updates and minor revisions to the Copyright Act were enacted in the 1800's.

1856 saw the Public Performance Amendment which gave authors the first right of public performance of their dramatic compositions. It also granted statutory damages for infringing this right. Recordation of assignments of rights was permitted. The invention of photography led to the establishment of copyright protection for photographs in 1865.

1870 Copyright Act

The issue of where authors should file deposit copies of their works had always been problematic. At first, copies were to be sent to the Federal District Court in the author's state. Later amendments designated the Department of State, the Smithsonian Institution, the Library of Congress, and the Patent Office as the custodians of the copies.

The 1870 Revision gave the Library of Congress sole responsibility to administer the Copyright Office and collect deposit copies sent in by authors. Librarian Ainsworth Spofford's political efforts made the Library of Congress "The National Library," and allowed its collection to grow through the free acquisition of deposit copies of registered works.

Copyright protection was extended to paintings, sculpture, lithographs, statues, and works of fine art. The registration procedure was simplified. Over 19,000 works were registered in the first year using new streamlined procedures.

1874 Print and Notice Amendment

- Notice simplified to read "Copyright, year, and name of author"
- Labels used on manufactured goods are not copyrightable, but can be protected as trademarks by the Patent Office

19ᵀᴴ CENTURY TECHNOLOGY ADVANCES

The nineteenth century saw the development of the typewriter (1826), the telegraph (1832), the color lithograph (1834), photography (1839), the Gramophone for sound recording (1877 and improved in 1888), motion pictures (1894), and the player piano (1897).

The invention of sound recording technology lead to the first exclusive recording contract with the United States Marine Band as conducted by John Phillip Sousa.

◀ "Washington Post March" 1890 – U.S. Marine Band
◀ "Washington Post March" 1989 – U.S. Marine Band

1894 First motion picture copyrighted in U.S. *Fred Ott's Sneeze*

1895 Lumiere brothers project motion pictures in public.

SIMPLE AND CERTAIN PROTECTION

The Copyright Act was amended fourteen times since 1870. In 1905, this led President Theodore Roosevelt to declare to Congress: *"Our copyright laws urgently need revision. They are imperfect in definition, confused and inconsistent in expression; they omit provision for many articles which are entitled to protection…they are difficult for the Courts to interpret and impossible to administer. A complete revision is essential."*

Congress took his advise to heart and completely revised the law with an eye to the advances of technology in the new century.

1909 COPYRIGHT ACT

- 28 year initial term + 28 year renewal = 56 years of protection
- Protection starts at publication
- Compulsory licenses
- Piano rolls are copyrightable, but not sound recordings
- Right of public performance for dramatic and non-dramatic musical works

- Notice of copyright is required for protection
- After February 15, 1972 sound recordings were copyrightable in the U.S.

🔊 "Maple Leaf Rag" 1916 – Scott Joplin

1976 COPYRIGHT ACT

Title 17 of the U.S. Code contains the copyright law. Effective January 1, 1978, it is the most fundamental revision in U.S. copyright law.

As Gutenberg's printing press forced changes in protections for authors; modern technology forces the copyright law to adapt. When enacted in 1976, the Internet, CDs, personal computers, MP3s, iPods, and digital downloads did not exist. It is the strength of the underlying principles embodied in the Constitution which allows the law to evolve.

Enduring Principles

As we study the details of copyright law and its application, we will examine how it adapts to changing circumstances. There are certain enduring concepts which never change. These are the main topic areas of this course:

- Subject Matter of Copyright
- Scope of Protection
- Exclusive Rights Granted to Authors and Owners
- Limits on Exclusive Rights
- Authorship
- Ownership and Transfer of Ownership
- Duration of Protection

- Formalities of Law
- Utilizing Rights
- Infringement
- Remedies for Infringement
- Fair Use

INTERNATIONAL TREATIES

Intellectual property knows no national borders. Just as Noah Webster had to register his copyright in each state, international authors faced similar problems. The end of the nineteenth century saw revisions in the copyright laws of England, France, Germany, Italy, and Spain.

The Copyright Act of 1790 only protected American authors. Foreign works could be printed or performed in the U.S. without the permission of the author. The United States became a haven for piracy of British works. In 1837 several British authors petitioned Congress for an amendment to protect foreign works published in the United States. Charles Dickens toured New England in 1842 and spoke for international copyright protection.

Gilbert and Sullivan's operettas *H.M.S. Pinafore*, *The Pirates of Penzance, Iolanthe*, and *The Mikado* were performed across America with the British authors not receiving a penny of royalties. They instituted several infringement suits, arranged for simultaneous publications in the U.S. and Great Britain, and sent their cast abroad under assumed names. This was all to no avail, for the courts determined that American copyright had been lost upon publication in England.

After *The Mikado's* New York premiere, Sir Arthur Sullivan thanked the audience and said: "It may be some day that the legislators of this magnificent country see fit to afford the same protection to a man that employs his brains in literature that they do to one who invents a new beer tap."

In 1886, The Berne Convention for the Protection of Literary and Artistic Works established uniform international standards for copyright. Although representatives of the United States attended the international conferences, the United States did not join the Berne Convention until 1989. Currently there are 136 member nations who reciprocally honor each others laws.

There is no such thing as an "international copyright." Instead, each member of the Berne Convention honors the copyrights granted under the laws of other countries. For example, today Gilbert and Sullivan would be able to sue American infringers in U.S. courts, simply by proving the validity of their English copyright.

21ˢᵀ CENTURY

As technology evolves, the copyright laws will evolve also. The fundamental principles and tensions addressed by the Constitution will not change:

Creativity is encouraged by copyright protection.

Society needs the free transmission of knowledge.

MODULE 03: COPYRIGHTABILITY

THREE ESSENTIAL ELEMENTS

In order for a work to be eligible for copyright protection, it must meet three criteria. It must be original, it must express an idea of the author, and it must be in tangible form.

A work which fails to meet any one of these three requirements, fails the test of copyrightability.

---

§102 Subject matter of copyright: In general

(a) Copyright protection subsists...in **original works of authorship fixed in any tangible medium of expression**, now known or later developed, from which they can be perceived, reproduced, or otherwise communicated, either directly or with the aid of a machine or device.

Originality

The definition of *originality* was deliberately left vague by Congress. Little is totally original. Creative expression builds on prior work. For example the piano only has 88 keys. Music is not just those 88 notes, but a combination of melody, harmony, tone color, and rhythm. Originality also requires the independent creation of a work, no copying of another work is allowed.

Expression

Copyright doesn't cover ideas themselves, only the *expression of those ideas*. Facts, forms, calendars, formulas, lists of ingredients, and short titles are not subject to protection.

$E = mc^2$ The idea that energy and matter are related is not copyrightable
but, Einstein's books explaining the idea are copyrightable.

The building blocks of language, music, and drama are free for all to use. Dramatists regularly use stock characters and plot devices in their screenplays. This technique is called *mise en scene*.

Fixed Form

A work is *fixed* in a tangible medium of expression when its embodiment in a copy or phonorecord, by or under the authority of the author, is sufficiently permanent or stable to permit it to be perceived, reproduced, or otherwise communicated for a period of more than transitory duration.

If it's not fixed, how can you prove it existed at all? Improvised jazz solos and comedy routines are not copyrightable until they are taped, recorded, transcribed, or filmed.

WHAT IS NOT COPYRIGHTABLE

The same clause in the Constitution which establishes copyright protection also establishes patent protection. Inventions are patentable, not copyrightable.

> **§102 Subject matter of copyright: In general**
>
> (b) In no case does copyright protection for an original work of authorship extend to any idea, procedure, process, system, method of operation, concept, principle, or discovery, regardless of the form in which it is described, explained, illustrated, or embodied in such work.

Facts are Unprotected

Facts are common knowledge and free for all to use. That Columbus sailed to the New World is a fact. Copyright applies to the way an author expresses that fact, in a book, movie, song, or painting.

Unfixed Works

Live concerts and performances, such as a live lecture or improv comedy skits are not copyrightable until put into a tangible format. Anti-bootlegging laws are used to prevent unauthorized fixation.

U.S. Government Works

§105 Subject matter of copyright: United States Government works

Copyright protection under this title is not available for any work of the United States Government, but the United States Government is not precluded from receiving and holding copyrights transferred to it by assignment, bequest, or otherwise.

Since the photo of Neil Armstrong on the moon was taken by an employee of NASA, the photo is a U.S. government work, and thus not copyrightable. MTV is free to use it any way they choose.

Municipal and state governments may obtain copyright protection for their works. For example, tourism advertisements and flyers are copyrightable in the name of the state.

Titles, Names, Short Phrases

Short phrases may be protected by trademark law instead of copyright, because short phrases and titles fail the originality test. The Copyright Office has registered claims to copyright in over 3,000 songs with the title "I Love You." Nevertheless, every rule has its exceptions especially when the title is indubitably original:

◀ "Supercalifragilisticexpialidocious"

CATEGORIES OF WORKS

The first copyright law of U.S. protected only books, charts, and maps. It has since been expanded. The categories of copyrightable works listed below are not a finite list, which leaves room for future technology. MP3s are not specifically listed, but no one argues that they are not sound recordings.

---

§102 Subject matter of copyright: In general

(a) …Works of authorship include the following categories:

(1) literary works;

(2) musical works, including any accompanying words;

(3) dramatic works, including any accompanying music;

(4) pantomimes and choreographic works;

(5) pictorial, graphic, and sculptural works;

(6) motion pictures and other audiovisual works;

(7) sound recordings; and

(8) architectural works.

---

§101 Definitions:

"**Literary works**" are works, other than audiovisual works, expressed in words, numbers, or other verbal or numerical symbols or indicia, regardless of the nature of the material objects, such as books, periodicals, manuscripts, phonorecords, film, tapes, disks, or cards, in which they are embodied.

"**Pictorial, graphic, and sculptural works**" include two-dimensional and three dimensional works of fine, graphic, and applied art, photographs, prints and art reproductions, maps, globes, charts, diagrams, models, and technical drawings, including architectural plans. Such works shall include works of artistic craftsmanship insofar as their form but not their mechanical or utilitarian aspects are concerned; the design of a useful article, as defined in this section, shall be considered a pictorial, graphic, or sculptural work only if, and only to the extent that, such design incorporates pictorial, graphic, or sculptural features that can be identified separately from, and are capable of existing independently of, the utilitarian aspects of the article.

"**Motion pictures**" are audiovisual works consisting of a series of related images which, when shown in succession, impart an impression of motion, together with accompanying sounds, if any.

"**Audiovisual works**" are works that consist of a series of related images which are intrinsically intended to be shown by the use of machines or devices such as projectors, viewers, or electronic equipment, together with accompanying sounds, if any, regardless of the nature of the material objects, such as films or tapes, in which the works are embodied.

"**Sound recordings**" are works that result from the fixation of a series of musical, spoken, or other sounds, but not including the sounds accompanying a motion picture or other audiovisual work, regardless of the nature of the material objects, such as disks, tapes, or other phonorecords, in which they are embodied.

An "**architectural work**" is the design of a building as embodied in any tangible medium of expression, including a building, architectural plans, or drawings. The work includes the overall form as well as the arrangement and composition of spaces and elements in the design, but does not include individual standard features.

Remember that the same §106 rights apply to any work which is protected by copyright. A photographer has the right to make copies and distribute her work just as a playwright has a right to control the public performance of a play.

Choreography

If you don't have a video of a dance, how can it be fixed? Rudolf Laban, (1879-1958) invented a system of notation to describe dance and human movement known as *Kinetography Laban* or *Labanotation*. First used in the theatre, Laban's system was applied to biomechanics and the movement of industrial workers in order to improve factory efficiency.

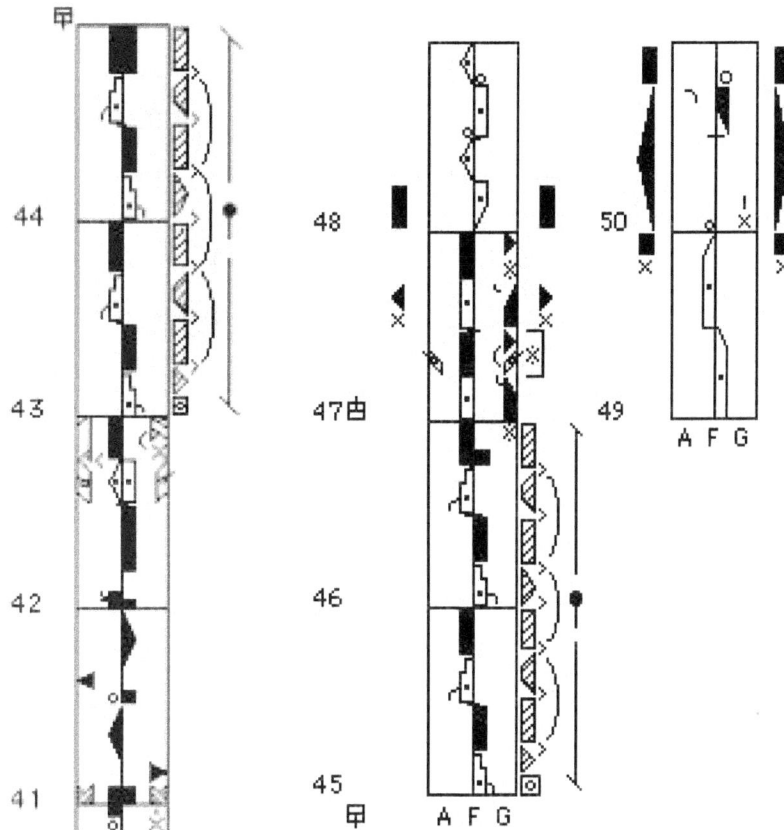

This is the notation for ten bars of *The March of the Waxed Fruit*.

NEW MEDIA

How did the Copyright Office handle the first movie? It met the three requirements of originality, expression, and fixation, but the medium was entirely new.

To test out his new invention, Edison put one of his employees in front of the camera. Fred Ott's party trick was performing a big silly sneeze. Edison's employee filed for copyright protection for *The Kinetoscopic Record of a Sneeze* created on January 7, 1894. The application was rejected by the Copyright Office because there was no category for motion pictures, as Thomas Edison had just invented the movie camera. This is another instance where technology advanced faster than copyright law.

The Copyright Office had been granting protection to photographs since 1839. They accepted Edison's copyright application later in 1894 when the deposit copy submitted was the series of individual photos pasted in sequence on a piece of cardboard.

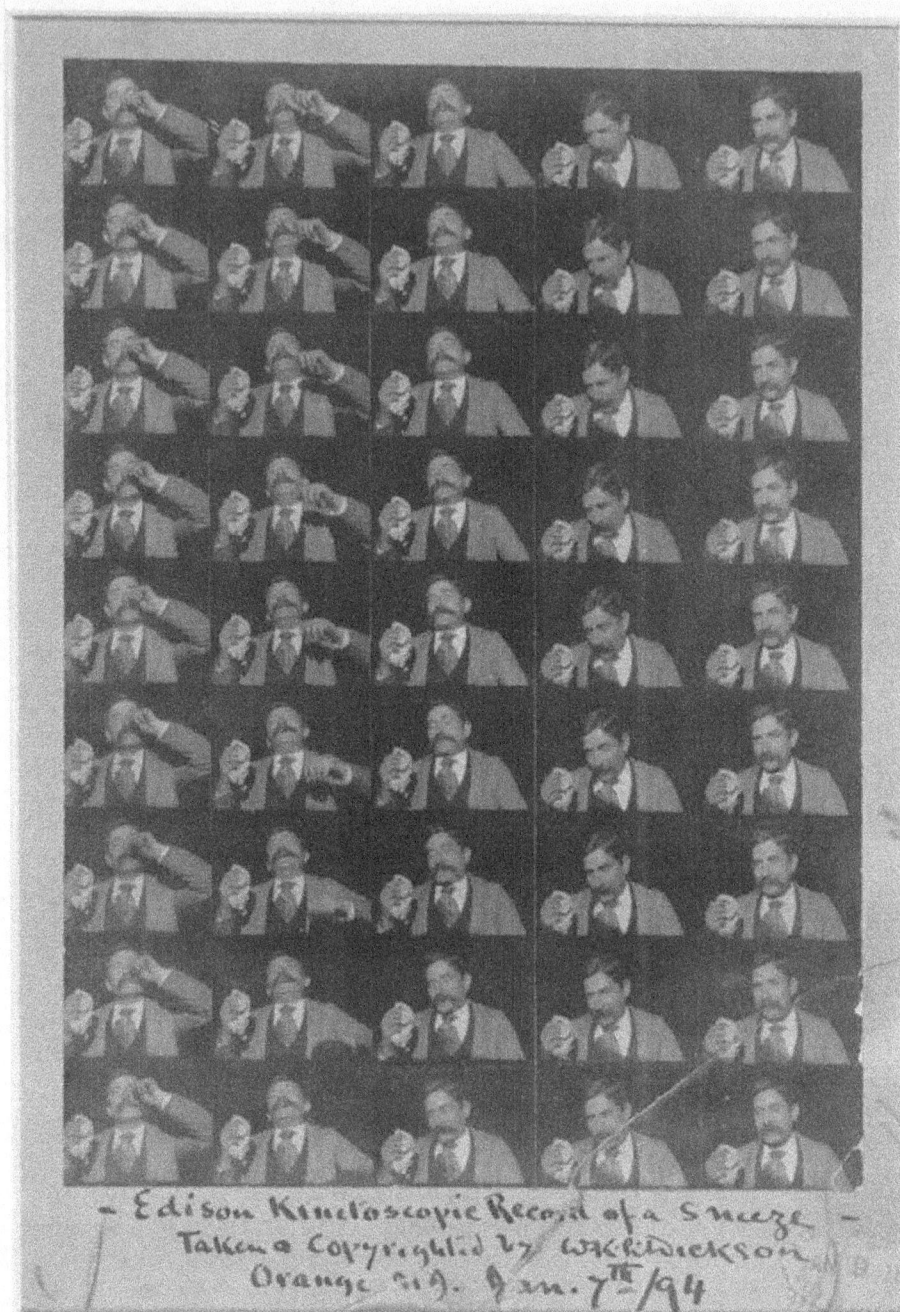

Fred Ott's Sneeze

The Copyright Act of 1976 clearly defines a motion picture and lists it the categories of works entitled to protection in §102(a)(6).

> **§101 Definitions:** "**Motion pictures**" are audiovisual works consisting of a series of related images which, when shown in succession, impart an impression of motion, together with accompanying sounds, if any.

Sound Recordings

Two types of copyright will be covered in this course. The copyright to a composition is owned and/or controlled by the author and/or music publisher. The sound recording copyright is usually owned and/or controlled by a record label.

Copyright notice for a sound recording is indicated by the symbol: ℗ as distinguished from the composition (sheet music) notice: ©.

CDs distributed for sale embody several types of copyrightable materials. The Form SR ℗ copyright protects the sound recording and a Form PA © copyright protects the underlying compositions. Another Form VA copyright may protect the photograph of the band on the cover. The liner notes are protected by a Form TX copyright. The © symbol is used for musical compositions, visuals, and text.

Any sound recording can be protected, not just music

- The spoken word
- A lecture
- Stand-up comic routines
- Sound effects
- The song of the whales
- Narration of a book.

Note that sound recordings too, must meet the requirements of originality, expression, and fixation.

A little known fact that you can use to impress your friends – until February 15, 1972, sound recordings were not copyrightable in the United States, but were protected under state property laws.

Compilations and Derivatives

Copyright can only be claimed in material which meets the three requirements of originality, expression, and fixation.

> **§101 Definitions:**
>
> A "**collective work**" is a work, such as a periodical issue, anthology, or encyclopedia, in which a number of contributions, constituting separate and independent works in themselves, are assembled into a collective whole.
>
> A "**compilation**" is a work formed by the collection and assembling of preexisting materials or of data that are selected, coordinated, or arranged in such a way that the resulting work as a whole constitutes an original work of authorship. The term "compilation" includes collective works.

A "**derivative work**" is a work based upon one or more preexisting works, such as a translation, musical arrangement, dramatization, fictionalization, motion picture version, sound recording, art reproduction, abridgment, condensation, or any other form in which a work may be recast, transformed, or adapted. A work consisting of editorial revisions, annotations, elaborations, or other modifications, which, as a whole, represent an original work of authorship, is a "derivative work".

§103 Subject matter of copyright: Compilations and derivative works

(a) The subject matter of copyright as specified by section 102 includes compilations and derivative works...

(b) The copyright in a compilation or derivative work extends only to the material contributed by the author of such work, as distinguished from the preexisting material employed in the work, and does not imply any exclusive right in the preexisting material. The copyright in such work is independent of, and does not affect or enlarge the scope, duration, ownership, or subsistence of, any copyright protection in the preexisting material.

MODULE 04: AUTHORSHIP AND OWNERSHIP

OWNERSHIP

> §201(a) Initial Ownership
>
> Copyright in a work protected under this title **vests initially in the author** or authors of the work.

The author holds initial ownership of copyright at the creation of a work that meets the requirements of originality, expression, and fixation. Automatic copyright protection begins at the moment of fixation. An easy way to think of it is that the copyright starts when the ink is dry, and the author is the one who is holding the pen.

Collaboration

A "**joint work**" is a work prepared by two or more authors with the **intention** that their contributions be **merged** into inseparable or interdependent parts of a **unitary whole**.

Each work need not be created simultaneously or at the same place as long as there is an **intent to merge**.

Original Score of Beethoven's 9th Symphony 4th Movement
which incorporates Schiller's Ode to Joy

AN DIE FREUDE	ODE TO JOY
(Friedrich Schiller 1759 - 1805)	

Freude, schoener Goetterfunken,	Joy, beautiful spark of the gods,
Tochter aus Elysium,	Daughter of Elysium,
Wir betreten feuertrunken,	We enter fire imbibed,
Himmlische, dein Heiligtum.	Heavenly, thy sanctuary.
Deine Zauber binden wieder	Thy magic reunites those
Was der Mode Schwert geteilt	Whom stern custom has parted;
Bettler werden Fuerstenbrueder	All men will become brothers
Wo dein sanfter Fluegel weilt.	Under thy gentle wing.

```
        ┌─────────────────────┐
        │  Joint Authorship   │
        └─────────────────────┘
         │                │
┌──────────────┐   ┌─────────────────┐
│  Intent to   │   │   Each Part     │
│ Collaborate  │   │  Independently  │
│              │   │  Copyrightable  │
└──────────────┘   └─────────────────┘
```

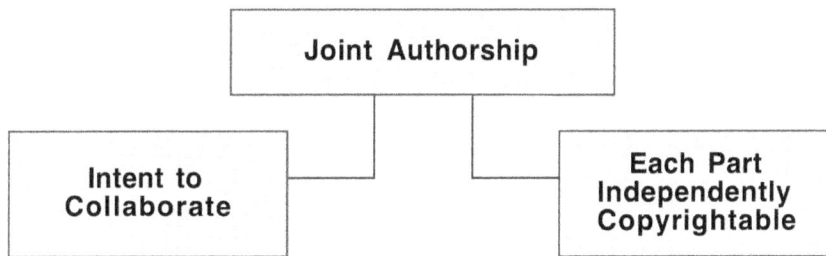

Before each independent part is merged into the whole, it must still meet the tests of copyrightability:

- Original
- Expression
- Fixed form

JOINT AUTHORS ARE JOINT OWNERS

Equal Undivided Ownership

> **§210 (a) Initial Ownership**
>
> Copyright in a work protected under this title vests initially in the author or authors of the work. The **authors of a joint work are co-owners of copyright** in the work.

In a joint work, the lyricist doesn't own the exclusive copyright in the words and the composer doesn't own the exclusive copyright in the music. Instead, each owns half of the copyright in the whole work. Joint authors are free to adjust ownership percentages any way they choose as long as the agreement is in writing.

Since each is a copyright owner, each can fully exploit all the §106 rights. There are only two obligations owed by the joint owners:

Duty to Account and Pay to Co-Owner

Each co-owner has to pay to the other(s) their share of income generated by the licensing of the work.

Duty Not to Destroy the Work

Since each joint author can license the work; there is a possibility that an income producing licensed use can destroy the value of the work.

Many songwriters prohibit their music publishers from licensing their songs for political campaigns or other products such as alcohol or tobacco. Since copyright lasts for such a long time, the potential always exists for the financial benefits of a lucrative short-term license to create a long-term negative association in the public's mind.

"I'd like to teach the world to sing" – "I'd like to buy the world a Coke." The popular hit for Melanie was licensed to Coca-Cola. Everyone knows the words to the commercial, but no one remembers the original lyrics.

In the 2004 election, the Democratic party released a special 2½ minute advertisement containing John Fogerty's Credence Clearwater song "Fortunate One." Does that overt political use of the tune for the Democrats harm sales of the song to Republicans?

What if your co-author licensed your joint work as the new theme for the Nazi Party? Does that destroy the value of the underlying work? Is the licensing fee worth it? This should be addressed in any joint authorship agreement.

WORKS-FOR-HIRE

§101 A "work made for hire" is

(1) a work prepared by an employee within the scope of his or her employment; or

(2) a work specially ordered or commissioned for use as a contribution to a collective work, as a part of a motion picture or other audiovisual work, as a translation, as a supplementary work, as a compilation, as an instructional text, as a test, as answer material for a test, or as an atlas, if the parties expressly agree in a written instrument signed by them that the work shall be considered a work made for hire.

Scope of Employment

- Was the employee paid to create a copyrightable work?
- Was the job performed during work hours?
- Was the job performed at the workplace?
- Was the copyrightable work created to benefit the employer?

> **§201 Ownership of copyright**
>
> (b) **Works Made for Hire.**—In the case of a work made for hire, the **employer** or other person for whom the work was prepared **is considered the author** for purposes of this title, and, unless the parties have expressly agreed otherwise in a written instrument signed by them, owns all of the rights comprised in the copyright.

Why is it important to determine authorship and thus ownership?

- Different lengths of copyright protection apply to author/owners and works–for–hire.

- Different rules govern transfers and termination of transfers.

- Who controls the copyright and thus the §106 rights?

- There are no termination rights for an author of a work-for-hire.

Community for Creative Non-Violence (CCNV)

The Supreme Court in *Community for Creative Non-Violence v. Reid* 109 Sup.Ct. 2166, 490 U.S. 730 (1989); addressed the question of "what makes an employee an employee" for the purposes of the work for hire provisions of copyright.

In the fall of 1985, CCNV, a Washington, D.C. organization dedicated to eliminating homelessness, entered into an oral agreement with Reid, a sculptor, to produce a statue dramatizing the plight of the homeless. While Reid worked on the statue in his Baltimore studio, CCNV members visited him on a number of occasions to check on his progress and to coordinate CCNV's construction of the sculpture's base in accordance with the parties' agreement. Reid accepted most of CCNV's suggestions and directions as to the sculpture's configuration and appearance.

After the completed work was delivered to Washington, CCNV paid Reid the final installment of the agreed-upon price, joined the sculpture to its base, and displayed it.

AND STILL THERE IS *NO* ROOM AT THE INN

Reid's sculpture

The parties, who had never discussed who owned the copyright in the sculpture, then filed competing copyright registration certificates.

The court held that the sculpture was not a work–for–hire since it was not "prepared by an employee within the scope of his or her employment" in light of Reid's status as an independent contractor.

The Supreme Court established 12 factors to determine if a person who creates copyrightable material is an employee or an independent contractor.

1. What skills are required to do the work.

2. Who provides the tools and materials?

3. Where is the work is performed?

4. What is the duration of the relationship?

5. Is the work done during regular work hours?

6. What is the method of payment?

7. Are assistants needed?

8. If so, who controls the assistants?

9. Is this part of the regular business of the employer?

10. Is the artist in business for himself?

11. Does the artist receive employee benefits?

12. What is the tax treatment of the hired party?

In this case, Reid was clearly an independent contractor and not an employee of the non-profit. He was a sculptor hired to create one piece. CCNV should have protected itself by having a written contract with Mr. Reid before he even started on the sculpture.

Oklahoma Natural Gas

On April 19, 1995, Mr. Lester LaRue was employed by the Oklahoma Natural Gas Co. as the Safety Coordinator for its Oklahoma City district. As Safety Coordinator, it was part of Mr. LaRue's job to investigate explosions and take photographs of the scene.

Mr. LaRue was in his office when an explosion destroyed the Murrah Federal Office Building. Thinking the explosion may have been due to a natural gas leak, Mr. LaRue drove to the scene in a company vehicle to investigate. Once at the scene, he began taking photographs using a camera and film supplied by the company. He took pictures of the overall scene, as well as of company crews shutting off gas lines. During this time, Mr. LaRue also assisted company crews by watching for dangerous overhead debris and by locating and shutting off gas lines. At least once, he reported in to the company's command center at the scene.

At one point, while preparing to photograph a company crew going into a basement area to rescue victims, Mr. LaRue noticed a firefighter cradling an injured infant. He took a photograph of the two, which became the well-known "firefighter and baby" photograph. It is instantly recognizable and an icon of that tragic day.

LaRue's photograph

The photograph was published in Newsweek magazine, and later Mr. LaRue entered into a contract with Sygma, a clearinghouse for news photographs, granting it worldwide syndication rights to the photographs. According to the contract, the photographs were to be distributed with the credit "Lester (Bob) LaRue/Sygma." OK Natural Gas did not initially object to Mr. LaRue's sale of the photographs; however, it did claim ownership of them a month later. The "firefighter and baby" photograph continues to be widely used as a result of Mr. LaRue's contract with Sygma.

Without his employer's permission, Mr. LaRue contracted for the manufacture and sale of T-shirts with the "firefighter and baby" depicted on the front. Also, Mr. LaRue contracted with another firm to produce bronze-like statues depicting the firefighter holding the baby. About 700 copies of the statue were sold or otherwise distributed.

OK Natural Gas discussed with Mr. LaRue the possible conflict of interest in selling the photographs for personal gain. OK Natural Gas sent Mr. LaRue a letter claiming its ownership of the photographs on May 18, 1995. LaRue refused to acknowledge his employer as the owner of the copyright and filed a registration form in his own name as owner.

The Court concluded that Mr. LaRue was acting within the scope of his employment as taking photographs was part of his job as Safety Coordinator; it was during work hours; he used a company camera and film; the Company paid to develop the film; he reported in to the Company throughout the day; and he never told anyone he was taking personal time. The Court properly applied the work made for hire doctrine, through which OK Natural Gas, as LaRue's employer, was entitled to ownership of the copyrights.

FIXATION

Since a copyright begins when an author's original expression is put into fixed form, there are only two types of owners, authors or employers.

The general rule is that the author is the owner as of the moment of fixation. The exception is that in a work-for-hire, the employer or commissioning party owns the copyright.

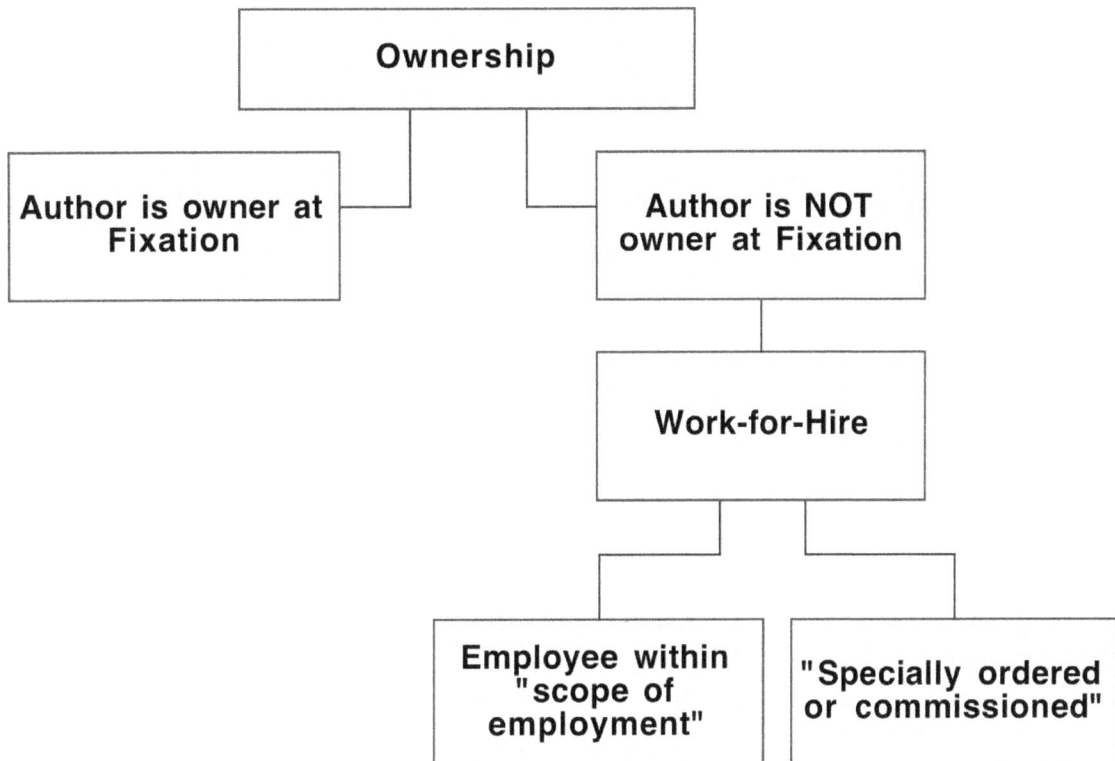

```
                    ┌──────────────────────┐
                    │      Ownership       │
                    └──────────────────────┘
         ┌──────────────────┴──────────────────┐
┌─────────────────────┐            ┌─────────────────────┐
│  Author is owner at │            │   Author is NOT     │
│      Fixation       │            │  owner at Fixation  │
└─────────────────────┘            └─────────────────────┘
                                              │
                                   ┌─────────────────────┐
                                   │    Work-for-Hire    │
                                   └─────────────────────┘
                            ┌──────────────┴──────────────┐
                  ┌─────────────────────┐      ┌─────────────────────┐
                  │  Employee within    │      │ "Specially ordered  │
                  │     "scope of       │      │   or commissioned"  │
                  │    employment"      │      └─────────────────────┘
                  └─────────────────────┘
```

MODULE 05: DURATION OF COPYRIGHT PROTECTION

HISTORICAL TENSION

The grant of exclusive rights to authors is in direct opposition to the value our civilization places on the free transmission of ideas. Copyright law walks a tightrope between the two and attempts to balance both concerns.

> **United States Constitution, Article I, Section 8**
>
> The Congress shall have Power...To promote the Progress of Science and useful Arts, by securing for **limited Times** to Authors and Inventors the **exclusive Right** to their respective Writings and Discoveries.

RESOLUTION OF TENSION

The stress between these two elements attains equilibrium in the Copyright Act:

Free exchange of ideas	v.	Incentive of monopoly profits
Protection for a limited time	v.	Exclusive rights
Life + 70 years	v.	§106 rights

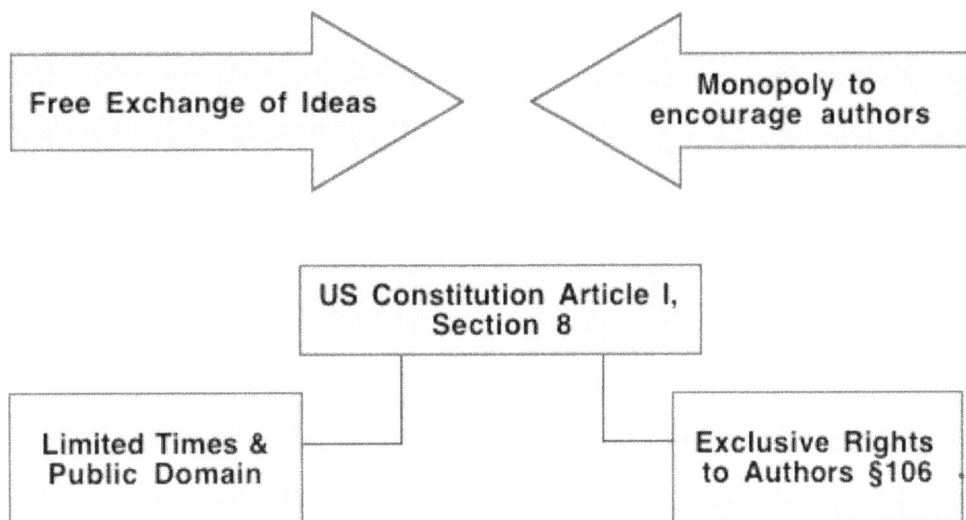

DURATION OF COPYRIGHT

> **§302 Duration of Copyright:** Works Created on or after January 1, 1978
>
> (a) In General – Copyright in a work created on or after January 1, 1978, subsists from its creation and…endures for a term consisting of the life of the author and 70 years after the author's death.
>
> (b) Joint Works – In the case of a joint work prepared by two or more authors who did not work for hire, the copyright endures for a term consisting of the life of the last surviving author and 70 years after such last surviving author's death.

Prior Laws

There has always been a recognition that the exclusive rights granted to an author under copyright must be limited in time. The following table shows the evolution of that time period:

1710 Queen Anne	14 years + 14 year renewal (if author is alive) = 28 years
1790 Act	14 years + 14 year renewal (if author is alive) = 28 years
1831 Act	28 years + 14 year renewal (widow can renew) = 42 years
1909 Act	28 years from publication+ 28 year renewal = 56 years

1976 Act (1/1/1978) Life of author + 50 years (no renewal)

1998 Sony Bono Act Life of author + 70 years (no renewal)

CALCULATING DURATION: AUTHOR IS OWNER

Under the 1909 Act, determining the duration of copyright protection involved checking copyright office records for the date of registration of the work, and to see if a renewal was properly filed. This led to inefficiency and confusion. It was often the case that a living author's early works were in the public domain, and thus he could not enjoy the fruits of his labor later in his life. The old method of 28 years + 28 years was scrapped in 1978, and the U.S. extended copyright protection for the entire life of an author plus a certain number of years after his death.

The method of calculating the length of protection for works created after January 1, 1978 is a straightforward matter. Only a few possibilities exist. Was the author the owner at the moment of fixation, or was it a work-for-hire?

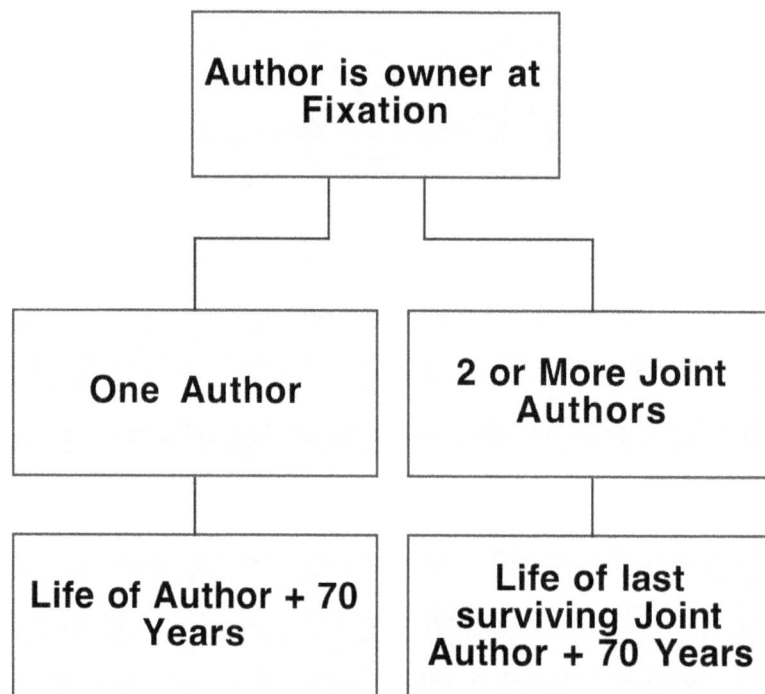

One Author

The copyright lasts for the **life of author + 70 years**

Two or More Authors

The copyright lasts for the **life of last surviving joint author + 70 years**

Joint Author Tricks

Some authors name their child as a joint author, thus expecting to extend the benefits of copyright protection by the life of their child + 70 years. Joint authors must intend to collaborate, and each joint author must contribute copyrightable material; namely something that is the original, fixed, expression of an author.

Year End

The law provides that copyright protection runs through December 31st of the 70th year after the authors' death.

> **§305 Duration of Copyright: Terminal Date**
>
> All terms of copyright provided by sections 302 through 304 run to the end of the calendar year in which they would otherwise expire.

CALCULATING DURATION: WORKS-FOR-HIRE

If copyright is claimed in a work-for-hire, the usual calculation of life of the author + 70 years *does not apply*. Often a corporation is the owner of the work-for-hire created by its employee. It is impractical to use the employee's life as a basis for copyright calculation. Instead, a different approach is used, based on the date of creation and/or date of publication of the work-for-hire.

When Was It Created?

That is, when was the original expression of the author-employee fixed?

Was It Published?

> "**Publication**" is the distribution of copies or phonorecords of a work to the public by sale or other transfer of ownership, or by rental, lease, or lending. The offering to distribute copies or phonorecords to a group of persons for purposes of further distribution, public performance or display constitutes publication. A public performance or display of a work does not of itself constitute publication.

When Was It Published?

The copyright in a work-for-hire lasts for **95 years after publication OR 120 years after creation, whichever is shorter.**

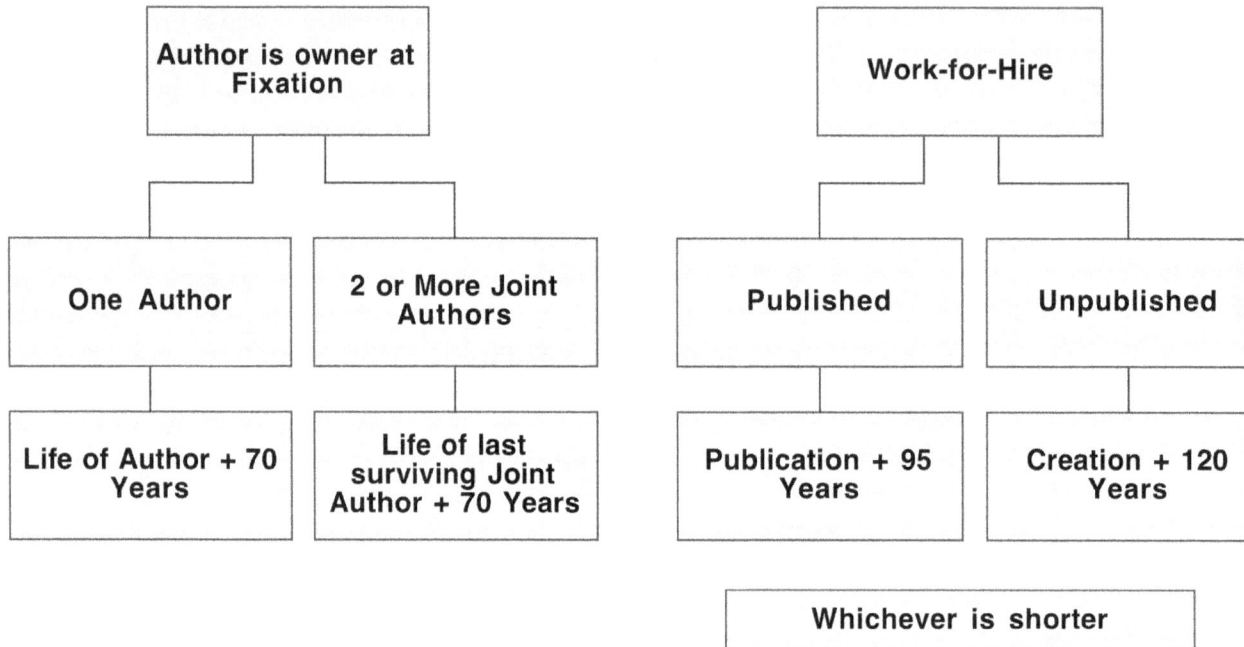

```
┌─────────────────────┐                    ┌─────────────────────┐
│  Author is owner at │                    │    Work-for-Hire    │
│      Fixation       │                    │                     │
└─────────────────────┘                    └─────────────────────┘
     │          │                               │          │
┌─────────┐ ┌──────────────┐            ┌───────────┐ ┌─────────────┐
│   One   │ │ 2 or More    │            │ Published │ │ Unpublished │
│ Author  │ │ Joint Authors│            │           │ │             │
└─────────┘ └──────────────┘            └───────────┘ └─────────────┘
     │          │                               │          │
┌─────────────┐ ┌──────────────┐        ┌──────────────┐ ┌──────────────┐
│ Life of     │ │ Life of last │        │ Publication  │ │ Creation +   │
│ Author + 70 │ │ surviving    │        │ + 95 Years   │ │ 120 Years    │
│ Years       │ │ Joint Author │        └──────────────┘ └──────────────┘
│             │ │ + 70 Years   │
└─────────────┘ └──────────────┘
```

```
┌──────────────────────────┐
│   Whichever is shorter   │
└──────────────────────────┘
```

MICKEY MOUSE

How long is a *limited time*? Can that length of time be increased or decreased by Congress? How much is too long?

> **United States Constitution, Article I, Section 8**
>
> The Congress shall have Power...To promote the Progress of Science and useful Arts, by securing for limited Times to Authors and Inventors the exclusive Right to their respective Writings and Discoveries.

Oswald the Lucky Rabbit 1927

Walt Disney's first successful animal star wasn't Mickey Mouse. It was a little guy few people today have ever heard of — Oswald the Lucky Rabbit.

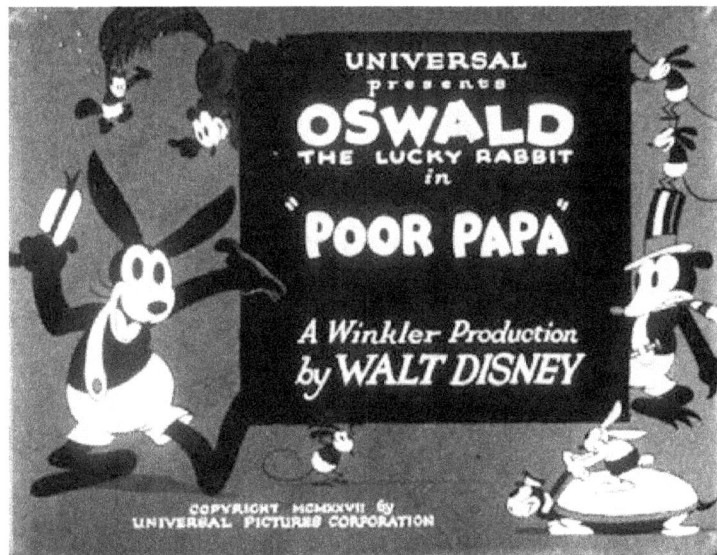

The first Oswald cartoon was *Trolley Troubles*, released September 5, 1927. Between that year and the next, Disney's studio produced over two dozen black and white, silent Oswald cartoons, which were very favorably received by reviewers.

Even then, however, Disney constantly strove for higher quality, and as a result, his cartoons became more expensive to produce. In 1928, Disney asked his distributor, Charles Mintz of Universal Studios, to increase his budget. Mintz refused and told Disney to accept a 20% cut in the budget, or he would hire another animator to do the work.

Rather than accept the pay cut, Disney resigned. Mintz gave the series to another studio who hired several ex-Disney animators to produce new Oswald cartoons. One of the animation director/producers was Walter Lantz, who is more famous for his work on Woody Woodpecker.

According to the official legend, Mickey Mouse was the result of a brilliant burst of inspiration which struck Walt Disney during a train ride from New York to Los Angeles. By the time the train arrived in Hollywood, he was ready to roll with Oswald's replacement. A more realistic story might be that he and key staff members, particularly Ub Iwerks, labored long hours to craft a new animated film star incorporating various physical characteristics they'd seen work in popular cartoons.

Mickey Mouse in Plane Crazy 1928

Whether Mickey was more a result of inspiration or perspiration, he first appeared in *Plane Crazy* (1928), and very soon eclipsed Oswald.

Plane Crazy

Steamboat Willie 1928

Steamboat Willie, released on November 18, 1928 was the first synchronized sound cartoon.

Steamboat Willie

Walt Disney, Ub Iwerks, and Mickey Mouse in the 1930's

Length of Copyright Protection for Steamboat Willie

1928	date of registration under 1909 Act
+ 28	years initial term
1956	end of initial term
+ 28	years renewal term
1984	end of copyright under the 1909 Act
+ 19	years Copyright Act of 1976
	(for works in their renewal term on 1/1/78)
2003	end of copyright under the 1976 Act
+ 20	Sonny Bono Copyright Term Extension Act of 1998
2023	Steamboat Willie enters the public domain
	after 95 years of protection

In January 2003, the U.S. Supreme Court declared that the Copyright Term Extension Act of 1998 was constitutional.

Happy Birthday To You

Perhaps the most famous song in the English language, "Happy Birthday To You" started as the simple ditty "Good Morning To You" sung in kindergarten. It was written by the Hill sisters in 1893. At some point in the 1920's, a second stanza with the Happy Birthday lyrics was added to the song. After an infringement suit filed by the Hill sisters, a court determined that they were the rightful owners of "Happy Birthday To You." The song was published in 1935 by the Summy-Birchard Corporation, now part of Warner Chappell Music.

1935	date of registration under 1909 Act
+ 28	years initial term
1963	end of initial term
+ 28	years renewal term
1991	end of copyright under the 1909 Act
+ 19	years Copyright Act of 1976
2010	end of copyright under the 1976 Act
+ 20	Sonny Bono Copyright Term Extension Act of 1998
2030	enters the public domain after 95 years of protection

MODULE 06: TRANSFER OF COPYRIGHT: OWNERS WHO ARE NOT AUTHORS

Under the Copyright Act, the author is the assumed owner of a copyright from the moment of fixation of the original expression of the idea. If the author is an employee or commissioned by another, the ownership goes to the employer as a work-for-hire.

TRANSFER OF COPYRIGHT OWNERSHIP

In the music business, it is often the case that the author is not the owner of a copyright. This transfer of copyright can take place many ways.

> **§101 A *transfer of copyright ownership*** is an assignment, mortgage, exclusive license, or any other conveyance, alienation, or hypothecation of a copyright or of any of the exclusive rights comprised in a copyright, whether or not it is limited in time or place of effect, but not including a non-exclusive license.

Types of Transfers

By operation of law	100% of all rights go by donation to another, or by will to the heirs
Assignment by Contract	100% of all rights are transferred, nothing is kept

Exclusive Licenses	Some but not all §106 exclusive rights are transferred
Divided Ownership	Transfer of less than 100% of the entire copyright

---

§201 Ownership of Copyright   (d) Transfer of Ownership.

(1) The ownership of a copyright may be transferred in whole or in part by any means of conveyance or by operation of law, and may be bequeathed by will or pass as personal property by the applicable laws of intestate succession.

(2) Any of the exclusive rights comprised in a copyright, including any subdivision of any of the rights specified by Section 106, may be transferred as provided by clause (1) and owned separately.

Transfers Must Be In Writing

---

§204 Execution of Transfers of Copyright Ownership

(a) A transfer of copyright ownership, other than by operation of law, is not valid unless an instrument of conveyance, or a note or memorandum of the transfer, is in writing and signed by the owner of the rights conveyed or such owner's duly authorized agent.

The simple reason why the law requires transfers of copyright ownership to be in writing is that by definition, a copyright will outlast its author. Duration of a copyright (which is not a work-for-hire) is the life of the author plus seventy years.

Transfers Need Not Be Recorded

What happens if an author keeps selling the same copyright repeatedly? The first to record his transfer in the Copyright Office takes priority. That is why even though a transfer is not required to be registered in Washington, it should be.

NON-EXCLUSIVE LICENSES

A non-exclusive license is a transfer of some individual §106 rights, but not all. The rights transferred may be licensed to others for different times, territories, formats, or uses.

For example a music publisher can license the same song to a Dutch sub-publisher for the territory of the European Union (EU) only and to a Japanese sub-publisher for Asia only. There may even be another license granted to a sub-publisher for sheet music print rights only. The owner's contractual obligation is to make sure that the rights granted to licensees do not overlap.

Sophisticated licensors can extract maximum value from splitting their §106 rights, but they must keep in mind that a non-exclusive license will always generate less income than an exclusive license.

The following chart shows how a single composition can be licensed. Section 201(d)(2) allows a copyright owner to split the §106 rights. Here they are licensed for different formats, lengths of time, and territories. Some licenses are exclusive, some are non-exclusive, meaning the same rights can be granted to another licensee.

§106 Rights	Format/Use	Exclusive	Term	Territory
§106 (1 & 3)	CD only	No	5 years	USA
§106 (1 & 3)	Sheet Music	Yes	Life of ©	World
§106 (1 & 3)	Vinyl & Cassette only	Yes	5 Years	EU & Rest of World
§106 (2)	Sync Television Ads	No	26 weeks	Selected Cities
§106 (2)	Radio Ads	No	18 months	North America
§106 (1, 2 & 3)	Sync Movie Theatrical	No	Life of ©	Europe
§106 (1, 2 & 3)	Sync Movie Home Use	No	Life of ©	World
§106 (4)	BMI Public Performance	Yes	10 Years	World
§106 (4)	Grand Rights (Stage Performance)	Yes	Run of Show	1 Theatre

BENEFICIAL OWNERSHIP

A **Beneficial Owner** holds the right to receive royalties from the use of a copyright, but does not own the copyright itself. Thus they are entitled to "benefit" from the income generated by the work. Not applicable to works-for-hire, beneficial owners may include:

- Songwriters under a publishing agreement
- Widows and heirs of authors who have signed publishing agreements
- Divorcees of authors (in community property states)

Community Property

There are a few states (notably Louisiana and California) which follow the legal concept of community property between husbands and wives. State community property laws hold that *"property acquired during the existence of the marriage, through the effort, skill, or industry of either spouse"* belongs to both the husband and wife. This conflicts with the federal Copyright Law which makes the author (not the author's spouse) the sole owner at the moment of creation.

---

§201 Ownership of Copyright

(a) Initial Ownership – Copyright in a work protected under this title vests initially in the author or authors of the work.

In other words, Louisiana law declares the husband and wife as co-owners of everything created or acquired during the existence of the marriage. Federal law holds that the author, not his spouse, is the owner of the copyright. In order for a spouse to be a co-owner, they must contribute copyrightable material or have a written agreement clearly acknowledging joint ownership.

Although this conflict of laws was brewing for years, entertainment attorneys never litigated the issue to conclusion for fear of setting an unfavorable precedent.

The Blue Dog Case

The conflict was resolved by the federal courts in 2000 in the case of *Rodrigue v. Rodrigue*.

To quote the court: "George and Veronica were married in Louisiana in 1967 and were divorced there in 1993. The Rodrigues' Louisiana marriage established matrimonial or community property. As a general proposition, the Louisiana Civil Code provides that, on divorce and termination of the community, each spouse owns an undivided one-half interest in former community property and its fruits and products."

"During the marriage, George became a widely acclaimed, highly successful, and very prolific painter. He created numerous paintings both during the existence of his marriage and after the divorce. A number of these depicted a stylized and easily recognizable image of a blue dog modeled after the family pet, Tiffany. George obtained certificates of copyright registration for some but not all of his paintings."

In court, Veronica Rodrigue argued that she was entitled to half ownership of all of George's copyrightable works created during the marriage. They each co-owned the family house bought during the marriage, why shouldn't the same thinking apply to the *Blue Dog*? Sharing the income from his art was acceptable during his marriage, but George argued that he shouldn't have to give his ex-wife co-ownership of his copyrights.

In a well reasoned opinion, the court decided that Veronica was entitled to a portion of the income generated by the *Blue Dog*, but since she was not an author of the work, she was not a co-owner of the copyright in the work. George still has the obligation to account and pay half the income to Veronica with an obligation not to destroy the underlying value of the *Blue Dog*.

Rodrigue v. Rodrigue, 55 F. Supp. 2nd 534 1999 U.S. Dist. LEXIS 2088; 50 U.S.P.Q.2D 1278 (1999), 218 F.3d 432 United States Court of Appeals, Fifth Circuit July 7, 2000 as revised August 18, 2000.

BUYING A COPY IS NOT BUYING A COPYRIGHT

Copyright is an intangible right. It exists independently of a physical tangible object. Section 106 gives the copyright owner the right to make duplicates. The sale of a book or CD is not the same as a sale of the §106 rights. Copies are tangible, rights are intangible.

---

§202 Ownership of Copyright as Distinct from Ownership of Material Object

Ownership of a copyright, or of any of the exclusive rights under a copyright, is distinct from ownership of any material object in which the work is embodied.

Transfer of ownership of any material object, including the copy or phonorecord in which the work is first fixed, does not of itself convey any rights in the copyrighted work embodied in the object; nor, in the absence of an agreement, does transfer of ownership of a copyright or of any exclusive rights under a copyright convey property rights in any material object.

TERMINATION OF TRANSFERS

The goal of the copyright law is to encourage creativity by granting authors exclusive rights. What if an author signed over a copyright in a bad business deal? Would he be stuck forever? NO.

---

§203 Termination of Transfers and Licenses Granted by the Author

...Termination of the grant may be effected at any time during a period of five years beginning at the end of thirty-five years from the date of execution of the grant...

Termination Requirements

- Not applicable to works made-for-hire
- Transfer or license of copyright was made after January 1, 1978,
- Author, or widow and heirs can terminate
- Earliest termination 35 years after transfer
- Written notice to the other party (2 to 10 years before termination)
- Copyright reverts to author, or his widow and heirs

The law provides a unique opportunity for an author (or his widow and heirs) to reclaim the ownership of copyrights after transfer. Why is the law so generous?

Under the 1909 Act, it was very possible for an author to outlive the copyright on his early works. Congress recognized that in switching from calculating the life of a copyright for a fixed length of time (28 year initial term + 28 year renewal); to the life of the author plus 70 years it was enhancing the protection afforded to the author, but simultaneously extending his pain if he entered into a bad deal. Under the old law, a songwriter who transferred his copyright to a publisher had the chance to recover it after the first 28 year term. He could renew the copyright for the second 28 years in his own name and strike a better deal with another publisher.

Under the 1976 Act, there was no equivalent renewal right, so Congress permitted an author to recapture his copyright 35 years after transfer of ownership. The notice requirements are strict in order to give music publishers ample warning that their license will end.

For a work created on January 1, 1978 (under the new law) and transferred that same day, the earliest date of termination would be the year 2013 (1978 + 35 years = 2013).

DONATION OF COPYRIGHT: PETER PAN

Since its first stage performance on December 27 , 1904, the story of Peter Pan and Neverland has been a part of childhood. The copyright to one of the best-known children's stories of all time is owned by a charity, the Great Ormond Street Hospital of London.

The Hospital first opened in 1852 and specializes in treating children's diseases. Since its founding, the Hospital has attracted the support of royalty, authors, and other celebrities. Queen Victoria, the Prince of Wales, several Prime Ministers, and Charles Dickens all contributed their money and efforts, but the most enduring support came from Sir J.M. Barrie who gave the Hospital its single largest donation, his copyright in *Peter Pan*.

Although he and his wife were childless, Barrie loved children and was a prominent supporter of Great Ormond Street Hospital for many years. In 1929 he was approached to sit on a committee to help buy some land so that the hospital could build a much-needed new wing. Barrie declined to serve on the committee but said that he "hoped to find another way to help."

Two months later, the hospital board was stunned to learn that Sir James had handed over all his rights to *Peter Pan*. Since then, the hospital earns royalties from every production of the play and every sale of books, videos, and other products.

On December 14, 1929, at Barrie's suggestion, the cast of a London production of *Peter Pan* came to the hospital and played out the Nursery Scene for the children, the first of an annual tradition. Only 5 feet tall, the man peering over the back to get a better view is none other than Sir James Barrie himself.

The Nursery Scene in "Peter Pan" was performed in "Helena Ward" on the 14th December, 1929.

In 1987, Parliament passed a special law which gives the Great Ormond Street Hospital Children's Charity the unique right to royalties from productions of *Peter Pan* forever.

```
                    ┌─────────────────────┐
                    │    Transfer of ©    │
                    └─────────────────────┘
                      │                 │
          ┌───────────────────┐   ┌──────────────────┐
          │ By Operation of   │   │   By Contract    │
          │       Law         │   │  (with 35 year   │
          │                   │   │ termination right)│
          └───────────────────┘   └──────────────────┘
              │           │
    ┌──────────────┐  ┌──────────────┐
    │ Inheritance -│  │  Beneficial  │
    │  Donation    │  │  Ownership   │
    └──────────────┘  └──────────────┘
```

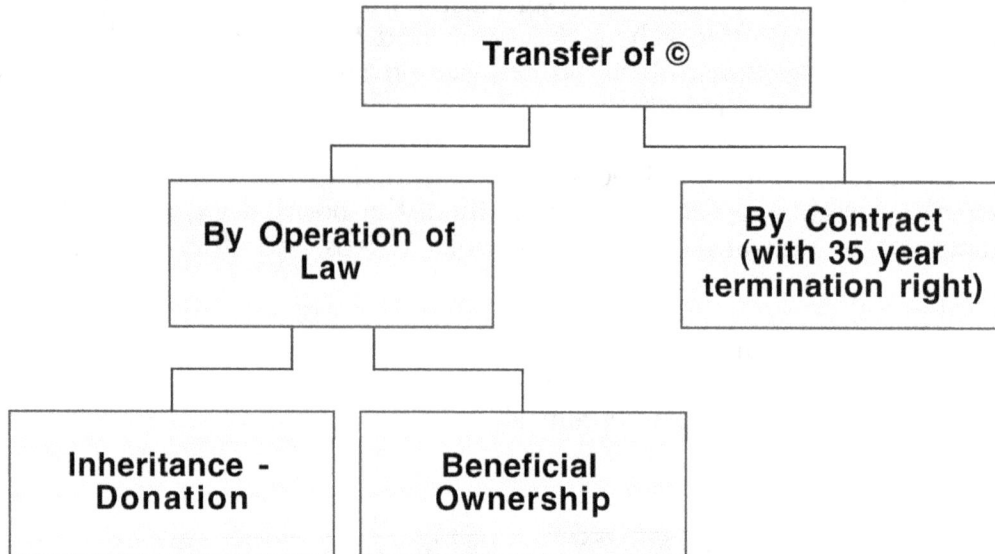

PUBLIC DOMAIN

The Constitution grants authors exclusive rights for limited times. Eventually all §106 exclusive rights end. An author's monopoly does not extend forever. If a copyrighted work – music, a photograph or a film – enters the public domain, it means that work no longer belongs to anyone and it is available to the public at large to use and/or to change in any way they wish, without any need to obtain permission or pay a fee.

Public domain is a one-way gate; once a work loses copyright protection, it can never regain it. Copyright is available only for the material that was added to a public domain work, and does not extend to the original public domain work itself.

Public domain means:

- The end of copyright protection of exclusive rights
- No one owns the work
- Free use by the public in any manner or adaptation

How can a work fall into the public domain?

- Copyright can expire
- Copyright can be abandoned by the author (computer freeware)
- U.S. publication before March 1, 1989 without copyright notice (©)
- U.S. publication before 1964 and not renewed

Famous Compositions in the Public Domain:

Alexander's Ragtime Band

Give My Regards To Broadway

Pomp and Circumstance

Stars and Stripes Forever

Way Down Yonder in New Orleans

In The Good Old Summertime

Take Me Out To The Ball Game

Silent Night

Auld Lang Syne

When The Saints Go Marching In

MODULE 07: PUBLIC PERFORMANCE

§106(4) PUBLIC PERFORMANCE – §106(5) PUBLIC DISPLAY

The rights to public performance and public display should be considered as twins. Just as a copyright owner has the right to make and sell copies (or refrain from doing so), the right of public performance and/or display is also exclusive to the copyright owner.

§106 EXCLUSIVE RIGHTS

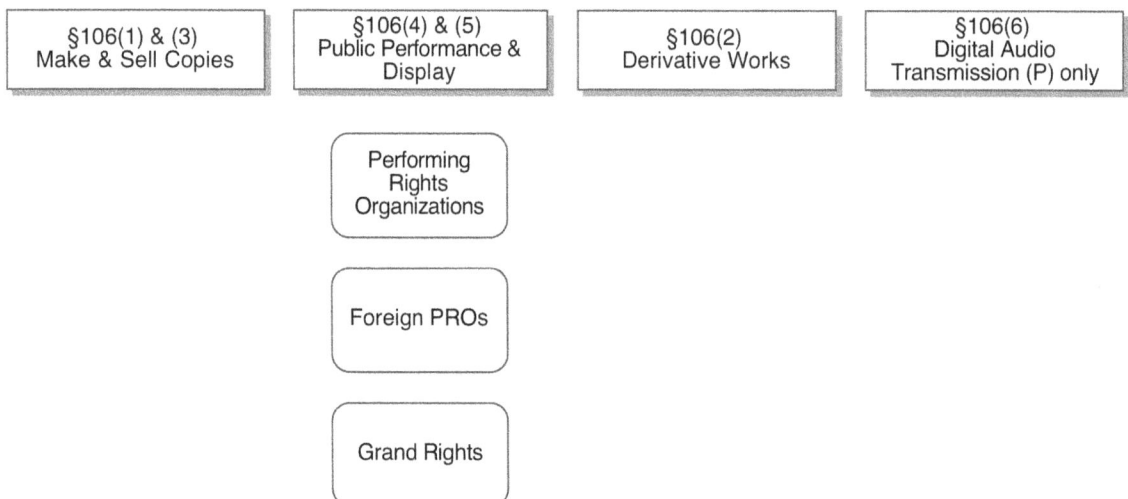

§106(1) & (3) Make & Sell Copies	§106(4) & (5) Public Performance & Display	§106(2) Derivative Works	§106(6) Digital Audio Transmission (P) only

Performing Rights Organizations

Foreign PROs

Grand Rights

Musical compositions are categorized as either *dramatic* or *non-dramatic*. The dramatic rights to produce an opera or Broadway musical on stage are called *grand rights*. Public performance of a song in concert, at a nightclub, or on the radio is considered a non-dramatic use or a *petite right*.

PERFORMANCE RIGHTS

A performance right is granted by the U.S. Copyright Act §106(4) to owners of musical works to license those works for non-dramatic public performance. Businesses which typically license the use of music include broadcast radio and TV stations, cable radio and TV stations, nightclubs, hotels, discos, and other establishments that use music in an effort to enhance their business. PROs are sometimes called "collection societies."

---

§106 Exclusive rights in copyrighted works:

...The owner of copyright under this title has the exclusive rights to do and to authorize any of the following:

(4) in the case of literary, musical, dramatic, and choreographic works, pantomimes, and motion pictures and other audiovisual works, to perform the copyrighted work publicly;

(5) in the case of literary, musical, dramatic, and choreographic works, pantomimes, and pictorial, graphic, or sculptural works, including the individual images of a motion picture or other audiovisual work, to display the copyrighted work publicly...

§101 Definition: To perform or display a work "**publicly**" means—

(1) to perform or display it at a place open to the public or at any place where a substantial number of persons outside of a normal circle of a family and its social acquaintances is gathered; or

(2) to transmit or otherwise communicate a performance or display of the work... by means of any device or process...

HOW DOES A COMPOSER GET PAID?

A Broadway musical play is simple to license, the music publisher issues a dramatic rights license (also called *stage rights* or *grand rights*) directly to the producer. In return, the producer pays a percentage of the box office receipts to the publisher who then pays the composer. In New York, it was easy enough for a publisher to walk down the street and check the ticket sales for each performance.

What about concerts in other cities? Harder to do, put its possible to have local agents issue licenses and monitor performances. What about dance hall bands? nightclubs? radio broadcasts?

It is impossible to monitor every song played by every house band in every nightclub. It is impossible to listen to every radio station 24 hours a day. Composers and music publishers knew that others were benefiting from the public performance of their music. Although the Copyright Act of 1909 had given them the exclusive right to public performance of their music, how were they to collect the money due to them?

PERFORMING RIGHTS ORGANIZATIONS

Performing Rights Organizations (PROs) act as agents for composers and music publishers by licensing the right of non-dramatic public performance to nightclubs, radio stations, concert promoters, and broadcasters; and then pay performing rights royalties to the publishers and songwriters of the performed works. The United States has three PROs: ASCAP, BMI, and SESAC. Each of the member nations of the Berne Convention also has its PRO.

---

§101 Definition:

A "**performing rights society**" is an association, corporation, or other entity that licenses the public performance of non-dramatic musical works on behalf of copyright owners of such works such as the American Society of Composers, Authors, and Publishers (ASCAP), Broadcast Music Incorporated (BMI), and SESAC, Inc.

There are thousands of radio and television stations, nightclubs, hotels, and amusement parks where music is publicly performed. It would be virtually impossible for individuals to monitor these music users themselves. Therefore, a PRO acquires rights from writers and publishers and in turn grants licenses to use its entire repertoire to users of music. A PRO collects license fees from each user of music it licenses, and distributes to its writers and publishers all the money collected, other than what is needed for operating expenses.

Grand Rights

A PRO only licenses non-dramatic performing rights. The grand right to perform shows on the stage must be obtained directly from the publishers of the music by the producers of the musical. PROs do not license mechanical and synchronization rights either; record labels and movie studios contact music publishers directly for these licenses.

For example, the grand rights for *Oklahoma!*, including Broadway, touring, stock, and amateur productions are controlled by The Rodgers and Hammerstein Theatre Library in New York.

ASCAP American Society of Composers Authors and Publishers

To solve the problem of unlicensed performances of their compositions, Irving Berlin, Victor Herbert, John Phillip Sousa, and Rudolph Friml joined in 1914 to create the American Society of Composers Authors and Publishers (ASCAP).

| **Berlin** | **Herbert** | **Sousa** | **Friml** |

Their solution was for individual composers and publishers to license their right of public performance to ASCAP. ASCAP would then obtain royalties from music users, such as nightclubs and radio stations under a *blanket license*. The licensee could perform any tune within the ASCAP repertoire an unlimited number of times for a set annual fee.

ⓘ   http://www.ascap.com/

BMI Broadcast Music Incorporated

BMI represents more than 300,000 songwriters, composers and music publishers in all genres of music. Founded in 1939, the non-profit company collects license fees on behalf of those American creators it represents, as well as thousands of creators from around the world who chose BMI for representation in the United States. The license fees BMI collects for the public performances of its repertoire of more than 6.5 million compositions - including radio airplay, broadcast and cable television, Internet and live and recorded performances by all other users of music, are then distributed as royalties to the writers, composers and copyright holders it represents.

ⓘ   http://www.bmi.com/

SESAC

SESAC was founded in 1930, making it the second oldest performing rights organization in the United States. SESAC's repertory, once limited to European and gospel music, has diversified to include today's most popular music, including R&B/hip-hop, dance, rock classics, country hits, the best of Latina music,

Contemporary Christian, the coolest jazz, and the television and film music of Hollywood's hottest composers.

While SESAC is the smallest of the three U.S. performing rights organizations, it prides itself on developing individual relationships with both songwriters and publishers.

ⓘ   http://www.sesac.com/

INTERNATIONAL PERFORMANCE RIGHTS ORGANIZATIONS

Most countries in the world have their equivalent PRO operating under their country's copyright laws. They have reciprocal arrangements with ASCAP, BMI, and SESAC for overseas performances of U.S. works, and U.S. performances of their members' compositions. Some of the largest international PROs are:

Australia: APRA

Belgium: SABAM

Brazil: UBC

Canada: SOCAN

International: CISAC

GEMA *Online*

Germany: GEMA

sacem f

France: SACEM

Ireland: IMRO

Italy: SIAE

JASRAC

Japan: JASRAC

Columbia: SAYCO

Netherlands: BUMA and STEMRA

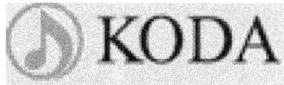

Denmark: KODA

Spain: SGAE

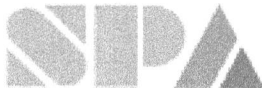

Portugal: SPA

United Kingdom: PRS

PUBLISHER AND WRITER AFFILIATION

Both music publishers and composers must join a PRO. Writers can only join one PRO, most music publishers have divisions affiliated with all U.S. PROs to service their ASCAP, BMI, and SESAC writers.

Writers and publishers grant their collection society:

- All of their rights to publicly perform and to license others to publicly perform, all or any part of their works, by any means or through any medium now known or hereafter devised

- The exclusive right to represent them before the United States Copyright Office

- The right to negotiate and to enforce the provisions of performing rights licensing agreements, or to withhold or restrict licensing in appropriate circumstances

- The right to collect performing rights licensing income from any source

- The right to allocate and to distribute royalties or other monies collected on their behalf

- The right to represent and to seek to advance their interests, along with the other affiliates, in connection with the rights granted herein, in appropriate forums, private or governmental, legislative, judicial, or administrative; both foreign and domestic

CLEARANCE

Every composition must be registered or "cleared" with a writer's PRO. For each tune, a separate registration form is filed listing appropriate information on the writers and publishers, percentage ownership, and any sub-publishers or foreign PROs. It is the job of the Index Department at the PRO to add the composition to its repertoire for allocation of airplay credits and royalties to the writers and publishers.

BMI clearance form

WHO HAS TO GET A PERFORMANCE LICENSE?

Anyone who uses music in their business must get a license, even for non-broadcast uses such as:

Airlines

Aquariums

Auto Racing Tracks

Baseball - Leagues and Teams

Basketball - Leagues and Teams

Body Building Contests

Bowling Centers

Boxing

Buses

Carnivals

Casinos

Circuses

Colleges and Universities

Community Centers

Concerts and Recitals

Conventions, Expositions, Trade Shows

Cruise Ships

Dance Clubs and Associations

Dancing Schools - Individual and Chain

Dog Racing Tracks

Dog Shows and Competitions

Educational and Informational Seminars

Festivals

Football - Leagues and Teams

Football (College Bowl Games)

Funeral Establishments

Grand Prix Auto Racing

Gymnastic Competitions

Hockey - Leagues and Teams

Horse and Harness Racing Tracks

Hotels and Motels

Ice Skating Rinks

Jai-Alai Frontons

Lacrosse - Indoor and Outdoor

Laser Shows

Local Government Entities

Local Municipalities

Motorcycle Racing/Motocross

Museums

Music-On-Hold

Nightclubs

Playgrounds (Indoor)

Polo Matches (Horses)

Professional Speakers

Private Clubs

Radio Stations - Local

Restaurants

Retail Stores - Individual and Chain

Rodeos

Roller Skating Rinks

Shopping Centers

Soccer - Teams and Leagues

Square Dancing

Symphony Orchestras

Taverns & Bars

Television Stations - Local

Tennis Competitions

Theme and Amusement Parks

Tractor Pulls

Train Cars

Volleyball - Indoor and Outdoor

Wax Museums

Wrestling

YMCA

YWCA

Zoos

THREE TYPES OF PERFORMANCE LICENSES

A *Blanket License* covers all works in a PRO catalogue. A radio station can play any ASCAP, BMI, or SESAC licensed song for an annual fee calculated as a percentage of its gross annual revenue. Stations must obtain blanket licenses from all three U.S. PROs each year.

ANNUAL STATEMENT OF ACCOUNT* BLANKET — FORM AB-96

PART 1 Account Information

*Report must be on Calendar Year Basis 19 ___

If less than full year Reporting Period ___ to ___ (Month Day Year)

AMERICAN SOCIETY OF COMPOSERS, AUTHORS AND PUBLISHERS
ASCAP Building
One Lincoln Plaza, New York, N.Y. 10023

Submitted by: ___ (Signature / Title / Date)

Type of Station: AM ☐ FM ☐

Accounting Method: Billing Basis ☐ Cash Basis* ☐ *Lic. 9E

If station is brokered by another station—enter calls ___
If all revenue to be reported by broker—check box ☐

FOR RADIO STATION:
Call Letters ___
Licensee ___
Address ___

Other stations covered by Report
Co-owned stations: (80% simulcast or <75,000 gross)
Time Broker for:

PART 2 GROSS <$150,000

GROSS REVENUE UP TO $150,000
If your gross revenue is $150,000 or less (on an annualized basis if the report period is less than a year) enter your GROSS REVENUE on Line 1 and the applicable LICENSE FEE from the Schedule at Right (pro-rated for any period less than a year) on Line 2. Your report is now complete.

REVENUE	FEE
$ Up to $ 50,000	$ 460
$ 50,001 - $ 75,000	$ 800
$ 75,001 - $100,000	$1150
$ 100,001 - $125,000	$1450
$ 125,001 - $150,000	$1800

1 Gross Revenue (excluding non-cash payments in goods and/or services) (Lic. P.5H) 1
2 License Fee 2

PART 3 GROSS >$150,000

3 Gross Revenue (excluding non-cash payments in goods and/or services) (Lic. P.5H) 3
4 Advertising Agency Commissions (Lic. P.5I (1)) 4
5 Revenue for Political Broadcasts (Lic. P.5I (2)) 5
6 Net Agcy. Comm. included in 4 above 6
7 Net Revenue for Political Broadcasts 7
8 Bad Debts (Lic. P.5I (3)) 8
9 Less: Bad Debt Recoveries 9
10 Net Revenue for Bad Debts 10
11 Rate Card Discounts (Lic. P.5I (4)) 11
12 Total Adjustments to Gross (Add lines 4, 7, 10 and 11 12
13 Adjusted Gross Revenue/Revenue Subject to Fee (Subtract line 12 from line 3) 13

PART 4 COMPLETE ONLY IF YOU ITEMIZE DEDUCTIONS

14 Total Itemized Deductions (from line 26) 14
15 Enter 11% of line 13 (Adjusted Gross Revenue) 15
16 Subtract line 15 from line 14 16
17 Revenue Subject to Fee (Subtract line 16 from line 13) 17

SKIP LINES 14-17 UNLESS YOU ITEMIZE DEDUCTIONS

18 License Fee (1.615% of line 13 or line 17 *but not less than 1% of line 13*) 18
19 Schedule: Compensation Under Lic. P.5J (1) (Attach additional sheets if necessary)

NAMES OF PERSONNEL | ANNUAL COMPENSATION

Adjusted Gross Revenue (Line 13)	Amount Not Deductible
$ Under - $ 50,000	$ 6,200
$ 50,000 - $149,999	$ 15,500
$150,000 - $299,999	$ 27,500
$300,000 - $499,999	$ 41,900
$500,000 - $749,999	$ 46,500
$750,000 - $999,999	$ 53,700
$1,000,000 and over	$ 62,000

Total 19

20 Amount Non-Deductible (see Table at right) 20
21 Deductible Compensation (Lic. P.5J (1)) (Subtract 20 from 19) 21
22 News Service (Lic. P.5J (2)) 22
23 Remote Pickups (Lic. P.5J (3)(a)) 23
24 Broadcast Rights (Lic. P.5J (3)(b)) 24
25 Other. Specify License Paragraph ___ 25
26 Total Itemized Deductions (Add lines 21 through 25. Enter on line 14) 26

A *Per-Program License* is used by broadcasters where music is a minor component of the program such as news, talk shows, and sportscasts.

ANNUAL STATEMENT OF ACCOUNT* PER PROGRAM — FORM APP-96

*Report must be on Calendar Year Basis 19 ____

If less than full year Reporting Period
____ to ____
Month Day Year   Month Day Year

AMERICAN SOCIETY OF COMPOSERS, AUTHORS AND PUBLISHERS

ASCAP Building
One Lincoln Plaza, New York, N.Y. 10023

Type of Station Covered by This Report

AM ☐   FM ☐

Submitted by:

Signature   Title   Date

FOR RADIO STATION

Call Letters

Licensee

Address

Other stations covered by Report

Co-owned stations: (100% simulcast)

Time Broker 100% for:

Fee Computation

1	Gross Revenue (excluding non-cash payments in goods and/or services) (Lic. P.5J)	1
2	Network Revenue for Programs of Licensed Networks (Lic. P.5K (1))	2
3	Advertising Agency Commissions (Lic. P.5K (2))	3
4	Revenue for Political Broadcasts (Lic. P.5K (3))	4
5	Less: Agency Comm. included in 3 above	5
6	Net Revenue for Political Broadcasts	6
7	Bad Debts (Lic. P.5K (4))	7
8	Less: Bad Debt Recoveries	8
9	Net Revenue for Bad Debts	9
10	Rate Card Discounts (Lic. P.5K (5))	10
11	Net Revenue Cleared at the Source (Lic. P.5K (6))	11
12	Total Adjustments to Gross (Add lines 2, 3, 6, 9, 10 and 11)	12
13	Adjusted Gross Revenue (Subtract line 12 from line 1)	13
14	Weighted Hours	

Enter Weighted Hours from Monthly Reports. Total and enter on line 14

Jan.	Apr.	Jul.	Oct.
Feb.	May	Aug.	Nov.
Mar.	Jun.	Sept.	Dec.

Total 14

15	Revenue per Weighted Hour (line 13 divided by line 14)	15
16	Weighted Hours Subject to Fee	

Enter Weighted Hours Subject to Fee from Monthly Reports. Total and enter on line 16

Jan.	Apr.	Jul.	Oct.
Feb.	May	Aug.	Nov.
Mar.	Jun.	Sept.	Dec.

Total 16

17	Enter 10% of line 14 (Weighted Hours) *but not more than 400*	17

Complete lines 18-22 only if line 16 is GREATER THAN line 17. Otherwise skip to line 23.

18	Multiply line 17 by line 15	18
19	Paragraph 7A (2)a. Fee (4.22% of line 18)	19
20	Subtract line 17 from line 16	20
21	Multiply line 20 by line 15	21
22	Paragraph 7A (2)b. Fee (2.135% of line 21)	22

Total lines 19 and 22 and enter on line 24. Then proceed to line 25.

23	Revenue Subject to Fee (line 15 multiplied by line 16)	23
24	Paragraph 7A (2) Fee. Enter 4.22% of line 23 *or* Total of lines 19 and 22	24
25	Paragraph 7A (1) Fee	

"Grandfathered" (Lic. P.7A (1) b) stations complete (a) for 1996 and 1997. All others complete (b).
(a) "Grandfathered" Stations

Adjusted Gross Revenue from Line 13	Previous Year's Adjusted Gross Revenue	Previous Year's	1996	1997
÷ x	24%	x	x x	x x

Total Enter on Line 25

(b) .24% of line 13. Enter on line 25.   = 25

26	License Fee (Total of lines 24 and 25)	26

| NRBMLC RADIO PER PROGRAM MONTHLY MUSIC REPORT - MUSIC LOG | | | | | | | | |

Call Letters _____

Account Number _____

BMI® — Please remit the completed forms to: Broadcast Music, Inc. Attn: Radio Per Program 10 Music Square East Nashville, TN 37203-4399 — Questions? Call (615) 401-2370

MUSIC LOG FORM MUST BE COMPLETED FOR EACH PROGRAM INDICATED ON PART 4 WITH AN "O" AS NOT KNOWN OR CONCEDED TO CONTAIN BMI FEATURE MUSIC.
* PLEASE ATTACH A COPY OF THE SOURCE OR DIRECT LICENSE CONTRACT FOR EACH OTHERWISE LICENSED COMPOSITION.

MONTH _____   YEAR _____

PROGRAM IN WHICH MUSIC WAS BROADCAST (AS REPORTED ON PARTS 2WD & 2WE)			OTHER-WISE LICENSED (SOURCE OR DIRECT)*	MUSIC PERFORMED IN PROGRAM	COMPLETE AT LEAST ONE OF THESE THREE IDENTIFIERS FOR EACH TITLE			
PROGRAM TITLE	DATE	FROM / TO (Indicate AM or PM)		TITLE OF COMPOSITION (Please Do Not Abbreviate)	PERFORMING ARTIST(S)	WRITER(S)/ COMPOSER(S) (List Full Names)	PUBLISHER(S)	BMI USE ONLY

PLEASE TYPE OR LEGIBLY PRINT ALL COMPOSITIONS IN WHOLE OR IN PART WITHOUT EXCEPTION   Page No ☐ of ☐

* BMI is a registered trademark of Broadcast Music, Inc.

The station must make monthly per-program reports to the PROs on these forms.

A *Source License* is granted to the producer of a film or TV program by music publishers. The music was "cleared at the source" by the TV studio. In this case, the PRO is supplied with a *cue sheet* that lists all compositions contained in the program, their composers, publishers, affiliations, and length. The cue sheet also designates whether the music is used as a title, theme, background, or visual performance.

When the program or movie is aired on television, the PRO allocates part of the broadcaster's blanket license fee to the composers and publishers of the music contained in the show.

Sample Television Program Cue Sheet

Title:	_____
Production Company:	_____
Original Air Date:	_____
Length of Film:	_____

Cue # Title	Composer	Publisher	Use	Time
1 Medley consisting of				
Signature	Jane Doe	Backbeat	BI	0:07
Juniper	Jane Doe	Backbeat	VV	5:37
Cowboys	Mike Roe	Apex	BI	0:34
2 Medley consisting of				
Juniper	Jane Doe	Backbeat	BI	0:09
Cowboys	Mike Roe	Apex	BI	0:45
Juniper	Jane Doe	Backbeat	BI	0:38
3 Boy and Bird	Irv Max	ABC	BV	1:25
4 Falcon	Bob Smith	ABC	BI	0:40
5 Medley consisting of				
Juniper	Jane Doe	Backbeat	BI	0:15
Signature	Jane Doe	Backbeat	BI	0:15
Cleo	Bob Smith	Happy Tunes	VV	1:25
6 Air Theme	Mary Loe	Apex	TC	0:30
7: Studio logo	Ruth Roe	XYZ	EE	0:05

Abbreviations:

BI = background instrumental	TC = theme closing
BV = background vocal	TO = theme opening
EE = logo	VV = visual vocal

LICENSE FEES

Broadcasters, concert promoters, hotels, restaurants, and nightclub owners pay annual fees to ASCAP, BMI, and SESAC for the right to publicly perform works by their affiliated writers and publishers.

Radio and Television

PROs use a complicated formula to determine the amount of the license fee a radio broadcaster must pay for a blanket license. BMI negotiated with all U.S. radio stations to receive the following annual license fee payments:

- 2001 $149 million
- 2002 $152 million
- 2003 $163 million
- 2004 $176 million
- 2005 $192 million
- 2006 $208 million
- 2007 $214 million (includes Internet streaming)
- 2008 $223 million   "   "
- 2009 $232 million   "   "

Each local radio station's share of the annual license payments is determined by use of a complex formula which factors in the total potential audience of the station, the average quarter hour audience as measured by Arbitron, and its gross advertising revenues.

Classical, college, and national public radio stations pay a lower fee than top 40 commercial stations. Radio stations which stream on the Internet or multicast digitally, must also obtain a license from all U.S. PROs. A similar formula is used for television stations.

Nightclubs

A nightclub owner's license fee is based on the annual entertainment budget for the club. This can range from $200 to several thousand dollars depending on various factors including the room's occupancy, whether or not there is a dance floor, and whether recorded music is also performed.

STATISTICAL SAMPLING

Figuring out what songs have been played on the more than 12,000 U.S. radio stations and in countless nightclubs is an impossible task. Since it is cost prohibitive to check each radio station and TV channel around the clock, the PROs use statistical sampling techniques to get a rough estimate of how often a particular tune was performed. This process makes many assumptions affecting how license revenue received is ultimately allocated.

PROs use electronic watermarks embedded in recordings along with the traditional DJ's log sheet to verify what song was played when. The size of the potential audience is a major factor. A spin on a 100,000 watt station in a large city is worth more than several plays on a small college radio station. Broadcast time of day is also considered. Morning drive time performances are valued more than late night plays.

Radio Airplay

About 750,000 hours are logged annually on over 12,000 radio stations in the U.S.

- BMI and ASCAP secretly tape radio stations

- SESAC uses Broadcast Data Systems (BDS) performance detection

- The PRO index department checks DJ's logs against tapes and BDS tally

- Each performance logged to a PRO member is multiplied by the ratio of stations logged to the total number of licensed stations

Television Broadcast

TV cue sheets are provided by film and TV producers to the PROs who cross check them against *TV Guide* listings. On TV, a feature performance pays more than a background performance. A guest band playing a song on *The Tonight Show* generates more money for the composer and publisher than a background use. Note that in the US, most sync licenses granted to TV and film producers include TV broadcast rights.

Nightclubs

ASCAP and BMI regularly send observers to nightclubs to log live performances, but more importantly to confirm that the club owner has purchased a performance license for his establishment. Look for a decal on the front door confirming that the venue has been licensed.

A public performance of a composition licensed to a PRO without permission is an infringement of §106(4).

Concert Tours

BMI uses an independent source of concert information to create a database which is used to track concert set lists and to determine which musical acts were among the 200 top-grossing tours. A royalty payment is calculated for each licensed work used in the opening and headliner's acts in each of these top musical tour set lists.

Since the number of licensed works changes from one semi-annual period to the next, as do the license fees collected from concert promoters and venues, the royalty rate for works performed in live concerts also changes each period.

Foreign Airplay

U.S. PROs have reciprocal agreements with foreign rights societies. If a French radio station plays a U.S. publisher's song, the French radio station pays SACEM, the PRO for France. SACEM then remits the performance fee to ASCAP or BMI who then distributes the money to the U.S. publisher and writer. The same process occurs in reverse if an American radio station plays a song controlled by a foreign music publisher.

DISTRIBUTION OF LICENSE FEES TO PUBLISHERS AND WRITERS

Generally, royalties for a single musical work, in any surveyed medium, are the product of this formula:

Number of Uses

times

Licensee Weight (size of audience)

times

"Follow the Dollar" Factor

(radio license fees go to radio performances - TV license fees to television performances)

times

Broadcast Time of Day Weight

(drive time is more valuable than midnight)

plus

Radio & TV Feature Premium Credits

(songs in heavy rotation get bonus credits)

equals

CREDITS

CREDITS x OWNERSHIP SHARE x CREDIT VALUE = $$$

2008 BMI credit values for ABC, CBS and NBC network television performances

	Primetime (6:00 pm)	Late Night (11:00 pm)	Overnight (2:00 am)	Morning/Daytime (6:00 am)
Full Feature	$11.50	$9.00	$5.00	$6.00
Theme	$5.00	$3.32	$0.58	$1.00 (Per Show)
Background	$1.10	$0.72	$0.52	$0.60 (Per Minute)
Logo	$0.30	$0.24	$0.22	$0.28 (Per Show)

What It All Means

Over a third of the money a composition earns comes from public performances of the piece. This means songwriters and publishers can rely on a steady stream of income from their works for the life of the copyright thanks to the efforts of ASCAP, BMI, SESAC, and PROs all over the world.

MODULE 08: REPRODUCTION AND DISTRIBUTION

§106 (1) AND (3) MAKE AND DISTRIBUTE COPIES

The most basic right under copyright law is the right to make a copy. But, what good is the right to make a copy if it is not coupled with the right to sell those copies?

First Publication

Implied in the right to make and sell copies is the *right not to sell*. In the music publishing business, this is called the **Right of First Publication**. Only the copyright owner can authorize the initial release of his work to the public. This issue also arises in recording agreements with record labels. If the record label owns the sound recording copyright ℗, then it has the choice to release the album or not.

Sheet Music and Folios

The origin of the music publishing business lies in the printing houses which engraved the sheet music of 19th century composers for sale to the public; the only source of income for composers in the 1800's. Today, sheet music sales are a small part of total income for songwriters and their publishing companies. This may change with the ease of downloading sheet music as PDF files from the Internet.

§106 EXCLUSIVE RIGHTS

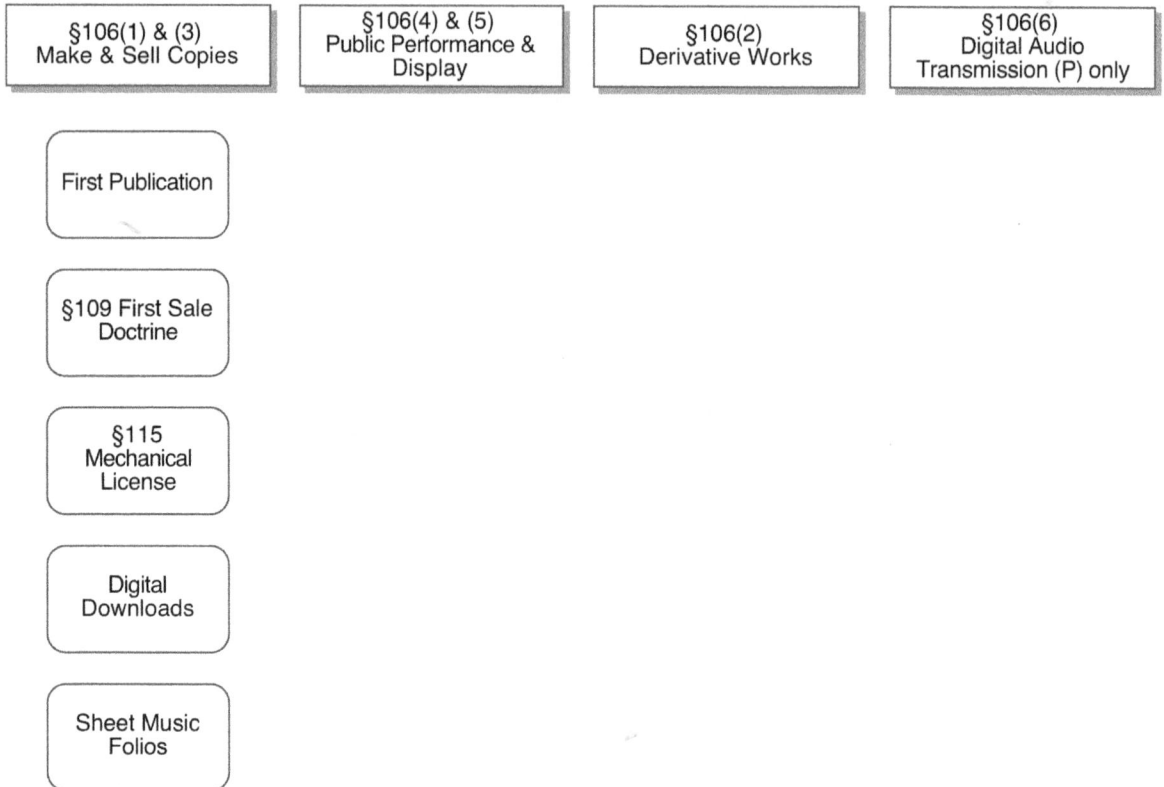

§106(1) & (3) Make & Sell Copies	§106(4) & (5) Public Performance & Display	§106(2) Derivative Works	§106(6) Digital Audio Transmission (P) only

First Publication

§109 First Sale Doctrine

§115 Mechanical License

Digital Downloads

Sheet Music Folios

§109 FIRST SALE DOCTRINE

Once a work has been released to the public, it triggers several important limitations on the rights held by the copyright owner. After release, the copyright owner still has his §106 rights, but has no say over further sales of the particular copies.

> **§109 Limitations on exclusive rights:**
>
> Effect of transfer of particular copy or phonorecord.
>
> (a) Notwithstanding the provisions of section 106(3), the owner of a particular copy or phonorecord lawfully made under this title, or any person authorized by such owner, is entitled, without the authority of the copyright owner, to sell or otherwise dispose of the possession of that copy or phonorecord.

After the copyright owner sells a copy of the work, the purchaser can re-sell it, give it away, etc. The ownership of the material copy or phonorecord is different from the ownership of the copyright embodied on the material object.

Consider the home video rental business. Movie studios often release high priced DVDs to rental stores earlier than their general release to the public. The *first sale* occurs once Blockbuster purchases DVDs from a movie studio. The video stores may then rent those movies several times to recoup their high price before selling used DVDs to the public. Blockbuster can rent or re-sell the video as it sees fit. The movie studio has no veto over who can or cannot rent the movie.

However, unlike videos and DVDs, no record rentals are permitted without the approval of the copyright owner. Rental of CDs would cut into sales of new CDs and no royalties are generated for artists and publishers for their rental or re-sale to the used CD buyer. The First Sale Doctrine is not applicable to illegal copies or illegal imports.

§115 THE COMPULSORY LICENSE

History of the Compulsory License

The first and most basic right under copyright is the right to make a copy. It is said that in the year 560, King Dermot of Ireland settled a copyright dispute between two churchmen over the copying of Abbot Fennian's *Psalter*. The defendant in that case, who was later sanctified by the Pope as Saint Columba, lost when the king gave his famous judgment: *"To every cow her calf and to every book its copy."*

For 1,500 years the basic concept has not changed – the original author or copyright owner has the exclusive right to make copies and publish the work. As embodied in §106(1) and (3), the right to make a copy gives rise to the whole concept of *"copy"* right. The author (or copyright owner) has a total veto over the first publication of the work.

Reflecting back on the tension between the grant of monopoly to encourage authors and the free expression of ideas, the Copyright Act has established an exception to §106(1) and (3). Although the copyright owner still has the right to copy and distribute his compositions to the public, *once a song is released to the public on a record, anyone can cover the song on their own record*.

The compulsory license allows new artists to record covers of compositions which have already been offered for sale to the public in phonorecords. This only applies to non-dramatic musical works released on phonorecords – not operas, not Broadway musicals, not videos, and not sheet music.

It is called the *Compulsory License* because the music publisher is compelled to permit cover versions. It is sometimes called a *Mechanical License* which allows for the mechanical reproduction of a composition on a phonorecord. It is also known as a *Statutory License* because the dollar amount of the royalty to be paid by the record label to the publisher is set by law.

§115 Mechanical License

After release of a record containing a performance of a composition, the copyright owner is **compelled** to allow anyone else to cover that tune for their phonorecords. There are only two restrictions:

- The cover tune may not change the basic melody, or alter the fundamental character of the work. The cover version can be arranged differently as long as it preserves the basic melody.

- The label that releases the sound recording must pay the composition's owner (usually the publisher) a fee for each copy made.

The maximum rates are set in the Copyright Office, but negotiation for a reduced rate is a common practice. Mechanical license fees are a large and steady source of income for music publishers.

The Copyright Act provides for a detailed and burdensome method of filing a Notice of Intention to Obtain a Compulsory License along with monthly pre-payments of royalties. It is the policy of the Copyright Office to encourage negotiation of rates between copyright owners and users. To this end, publishers and labels use their own mechanical licenses. If you notice in the example below, the label (Licensee) is relieved of the obligation to file a notice in the Copyright Office and has to pay the fees quarterly instead of monthly.

¾ Rate

It is a standard practice in the industry for publishers to grant mechanical licenses at **75% of the prevailing statutory rate**. This has advantages for both sides. First of all, the label saves money and effort. These savings go straight to the bottom line, thus increasing profitability of the CD. Secondly, publishers make covering one of their tunes attractive by offering it to the label at the reduced **3/4 rate**.

A §115 compulsory license only affects phonorecords released in the United States. Foreign countries have different ways of calculating and collecting mechanical royalties for their composers and publishers.

Sample Mechanical License

License Date: _____, 20__

Licensee: Record Label

Licensor: Music Publisher

Composition: _____

Writer(s)   _____

Timing: _____:_____ (minutes : seconds)

Statutory Rate: _____ cents per copy made

Cover Artist: _____

Record #:   _____

Release Date: _____, 20__

1. Publisher warrants and represents that:

     (a) it is the owner of a valid United States copyright in the above musical composition (the "Composition"),

     (b) the Composition is original and does not violate or infringe upon the rights of any person, firm or other entity,

     (c) it has full right, power and authority to grant this license and

     (d) it will be responsible for payment of all sums due to the writer(s) of the Composition by reason of Licensee's exercise of the rights granted hereunder.

2. Publisher grants to Licensee the nonexclusive right, privilege and license, irrevocable during the term of the copyright, to reproduce the Composition in phonorecords, to be manufactured and sold for distribution in the United States (the "Territory"), including the right to reproduce the lyrics of the Composition on the packaging of such phonorecords.

3. Licensee shall pay to Publisher copyright royalties at 75% percent of the statutory rate for each phonorecord containing the Composition which is manufactured and sold by Licensee for distribution in the Territory and not returned.

4. This license is intended to cover and is limited to the recording of the Composition by the above artist on the above phonorecord.

5. Licensee shall render to Publisher quarterly statements of royalties payable hereunder, within forty-five (45) days after the end of each calendar quarter, together with payment of all royalties due.

6. Publisher does hereby indemnify, save and hold Licensee harmless from any and all loss or damage arising out of or connected with any claim by a third party which is inconsistent with Publisher's warranties and representations contained herein.

7. This agreement shall inure to the benefit and be binding upon the parties hereto and their respective heirs, legal representatives, successors and assigns. The execution of this agreement shall constitute and is accepted by Publisher as full compliance with all obligations of Licensee to Publisher, statutory and otherwise, arising from or connected with Licensee's use of the Composition as provided herein.

Licensor: _____   Licensee: _____
    Music Publisher   Record Label

The Harry Fox Agency

Many music publishers have thousands of compositions earning mechanical royalty income. Some publishers use the *Harry Fox Agency* to issue mechanical licenses to record labels. Harry Fox charges its music publisher clients a small administrative fee for this service and also regularly audits record labels and CD pressing plants on their behalf.

It is also more convenient for a record label to send all of its requests for mechanical licenses to one place instead of tracking down individual publishers.

Harry Fox Mechanical License Request Form

hfa The Harry Fox Agency, Inc., 601 West 26th Street, 5th Floor, New York, NY 10001

Mechanical License Request
(*First Time Licensees Need to Complete New Account Form*)

Anticipated Quantity of Units ___ Over 2500 ___ 2500 or Under
Failure to check one will delay processing

Record Company/Licensee Name _____

Date _____/_____/_____

Address _____

Contact Name _____

Fax _____

City _____ **State** _____ **Zip** _____

Telephone _____

Title (One Per Form): _____

Writers: _____

Publisher(s) *(one per line)*	Percentage
_____	___ %
_____	___ %
_____	___ %
_____	___ %
_____	___ %

For Manufactures of Over 2500 Units

Song #

M				

Catalog Number-Album

CD_____ Cass_____ Midi_____ LP_____ Digital Comp Cass_____

Minidisk_____ MiniCass_____ DAT_____

Catalog Number-Single

CD single_____ Cassingle_____ Minidisk_____ 12" Single_____ Midi_____

DAT_____ MaxiCass_____ MiniCass_____ 17" Single _____

Rate: Statutory ___ Other _____

Label: _____

Playing Time _____ **Release Date** _____/_____/_____

UPC _____

Artist _____

ISRC _____

Album Title _____

Explanation _____

Publishers Approval _____

****PLEASE BE SURE TO COMPLETE ALL APPLICABLE FIELDS****

The Statutory Rate

Since the passage of the Copyright Act of 1976, the mechanical license rate has soared, making the formerly sleepy business of music publishing into a powerhouse that generates enormous and steady profits.

Note that for compositions longer than 5 minutes, a "cents-per-minute" rate is used. This is known as the "long-song formula."

§115 Statutory Mechanical Royalty Rates

year	¢ per-song rate	¢ per minute rate	change from 1909 rate
1909	2.00 ¢	none	n/a
1978	2.75 ¢	½ ¢	38%
1980	4.00 ¢	¾ ¢	100%
1984	4.50 ¢	.8 ¢	125%
1986	5.00 ¢	.95 ¢	150%
1988	5.25 ¢	1 ¢	163%
1990	5.70 ¢	1.1 ¢	185%
1992	6.25 ¢	1.2 ¢	213%
1994	6.60 ¢	1 ¼ ¢	230%
1996	6.95 ¢	1.3 ¢	248%
1998	7.10 ¢	1.35 ¢	255%
2000	7.55 ¢	1.45 ¢	278%
2002	8.00 ¢	1.55 ¢	300%
2004	8.50 ¢	1.65 ¢	325%
2006 to date	**9.10 ¢**	**1 ¾ ¢**	**355%**

MODULE 09: THE DERIVATIVE RIGHT

§106 (2) Derivatives

The right to make a derivative work which re-casts the original is an opportunity for an author to re-arrange his original work into other uses. For music publishers, derivatives include putting compositions into movies and TV shows (synchronization), changing the lyrics for translations, parody, or advertisements, and other uses. Likewise a record label can license its sound recording to a movie studio (master use license) or re-mix a release for different markets (street mix, dance mix).

> **§101 Definition**
>
> A **derivative work** is a work based upon one or more pre-existing works, such as a translation, musical arrangement, dramatization, fictionalization, motion picture version, sound recording, art reproduction, abridgment, condensation, or any other form in which a work may be recast, transformed, or adapted. A work consisting of editorial revisions, annotations, elaborations, or other modifications, which, as a whole, represent an original work of authorship, is a "derivative work".

§106 EXCLUSIVE RIGHTS

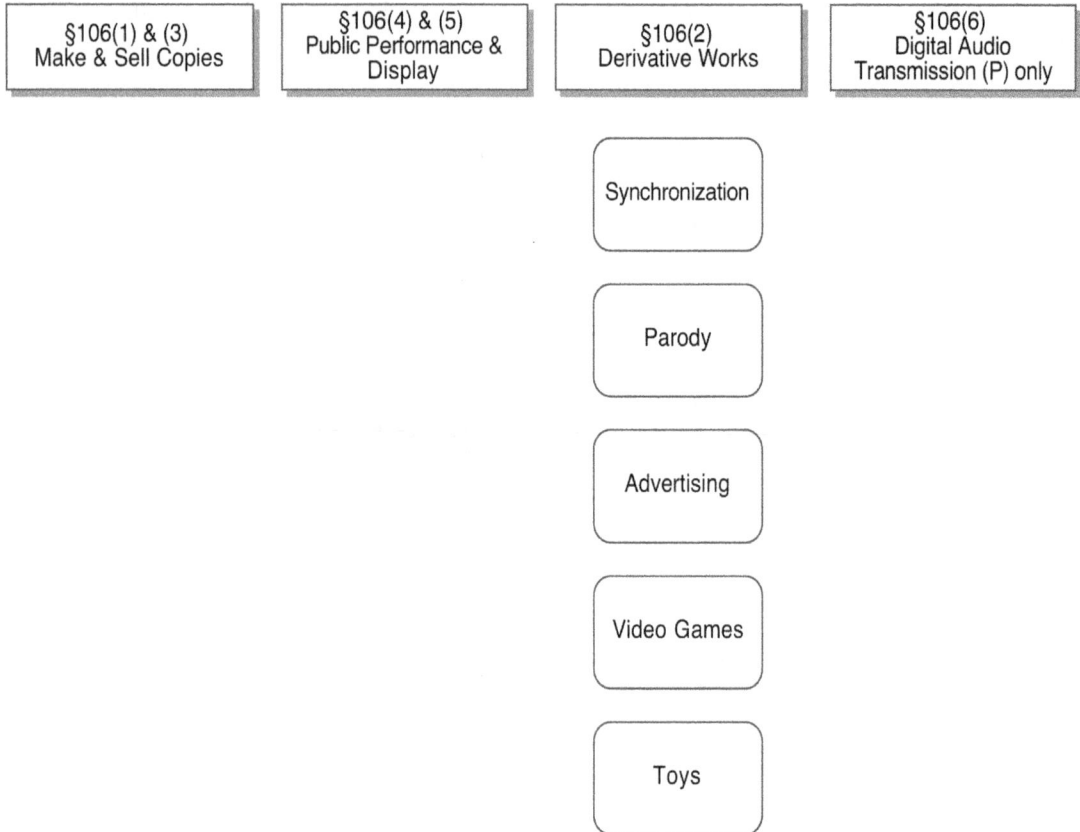

§106(1) & (3) Make & Sell Copies	§106(4) & (5) Public Performance & Display	§106(2) Derivative Works	§106(6) Digital Audio Transmission (P) only

Synchronization

Parody

Advertising

Video Games

Toys

17 USC §106(2) grants the copyright owner the exclusive right to make derivatives. Derivatives made without permission are infringements.

Requirements for a copyrightable derivative work

- Must borrow from another work
- Must transform or adapt the original work
- Enough has to be added so that the new material would entitle the creator to a copyright
- Thus the new material must be an original, tangible, expression of an author's idea

Examples of Derivatives

piano arrangements of symphony	Liszt arranged Beethoven's 9th
translations into other languages	Luther translated the Bible into German
M*A*S*H	novel – movie – television series
posters of paintings & artworks	recast into a new medium
Readers Digest Condensed Editions	editorial revisions & adaptations
Re-mixes of sound recordings	dance, radio, & street mixes
fictionalization	*In Cold Blood* by Truman Capote novel based on a real murder & newspaper reports

The copyright in the derivative extends only to the new material added to the original by permission of the copyright owner. You can't extend a copyright forever by creating derivatives based on derivatives based on derivatives.

---

§103(b) Compilations and derivative works

The copyright in a compilation or derivative work extends only to the material contributed by the author of such work, as distinguished from the preexisting material. The copyright in such work is independent of, and does not affect or enlarge the scope, duration, ownership, or subsistence of, any copyright protection in the preexisting material.

ARRANGEMENTS OF MUSICAL WORKS

Arrangements usually are not original enough to earn copyrightability, for there is a limited musical vocabulary available to arrangers. However, be aware that substantial changes to the original work made in arrangements may lead to the creation of a derivative work. In that case, the owner of the original must approve the changes.

It is possible to obtain protection in a derivative of a public domain work. For example, sheet music arrangements of public domain works are protected. Jimi Hendrix wrote an arrangement of the "Star Spangled Banner" – very original and thus his contribution is a copyrightable derivative based on a public domain work.

Musical Examples of Derivative Works

Candle in the Wind

Music by Elton John
Lyrics by Bernie Taupin

Goodbye Norma Jean
Though I never knew you at all
You had the grace to hold yourself
While those around you crawled
They crawled out of the woodwork
And they whispered into your brain
They set you on the treadmill
And they made you change your name

And it seems to me you lived your life
Like a candle in the wind
Never knowing who to cling to
When the rain set in
And I would have liked to have known you
But I was just a kid
Your candle burned out long before
Your legend ever did

Loneliness was tough
The toughest role you ever played
Hollywood created a superstar
And pain was the price you paid
Even when you died
Oh the press still hounded you
All the papers had to say
Was that Marilyn was found in the nude

Goodbye Norma Jean
From the young man in the 22nd row
Who sees you as something as more than
sexual
More than just our Marilyn Monroe

Music by Elton John
Lyrics by Bernie Taupin
Performed at Princess Diana's funeral 9/6/1997.

Goodbye England's Rose
May you ever grow in our hearts
You were the grace that placed itself
Where lives were torn apart
You called out to our country
And you whispered to those in pain
Now you belong to heaven
And the stars spell out your name
And it seems to me you lived your life
Like a candle in the wind
Never fading with the sunset
When the rain set in
And your footsteps will always fall here
Along England's greenest hills
Your candle's burned out long before
Your legend ever will
Loveliness we've lost
These empty days without your smile
This torch we'll always carry
For our nation's golden child
And even though we try
The truth brings us to tears
All our words cannot express
The joy you brought us through the years
Goodbye England's Rose
May you ever grow in our hearts
You were the grace that placed itself
Where lives were torn apart
Goodbye England's Rose
From a country lost without your soul
Who'll miss the wings of your compassion
More than you'll ever know
And it seems to me you lived your life
Like a candle in the wind
Never fading with the sunset
When the rain set in
And your footsteps will always fall here
Along England's greenest hills
Your candle's burned out long before
Your legend ever will

Same tune – different lyrics. Elton John and Bernie Taupin are the original authors therefore they have the right to make a derivative.

🔊 "Candle in the Wind" (Goodbye Norma Jean)

🔊 "Candle in the Wind" (Princess Diana)

Unforgettable

Nat "King" Cole recorded the original version on Capitol Records which hit a peak Billboard position #12 in 1951-52. It was covered and charted in 1954 by the Dick Hyman Trio (#29), and also in 1959 by Dinah Washington (#17).

In 1991 derivative of the original sound recording was re-mixed by producer Andre Fisher with additional vocals by Natalie Cole. It won 3 Grammy awards in 1992, Album of the Year, Record of the Year, and Song of the Year (for composer Irving Gordon).

🔊 "Unforgettable" (original 1951)

🔊 "Unforgettable" (duet 1991)

Every Breath You Take

Change in the intent of the tune makes it a derivative. If Puff Daddy had just said "I'm going to sing a song in memory of Notorious B.I.G. – then it's not a derivative.

Every Breath You Take
by Sting

Every breath you take
Every move you make
Every bond you break
Every step you take
I'll be watching you

Every single day
Every word you say
Every game you play
Every night you stay
I'll be watching you

Oh, can't you see
You belong to me
How my poor heart aches
With every step you take

Every move you make
Every vow you break
Every smile you fake
Every claim you stake
I'll be watching you

Since you've gone I've been lost without a trace
I dream at night I can only see your face
I look around but it's you I can't replace
I feel so cold and I long for your embrace
I keep crying baby, baby, please...

Oh, can't you see
You belong to me
How my poor heart aches
With every breath you take

Every move you make
Every vow you break
Every smile you fake
Every claim you stake
I'll be watching you

Every move you make
Every step you take
I'll be watching you...

◀ "Every Breath You Take" – The Police

◀ "Every Breath You Take" – Puff Daddy Video Music Awards

99 Red Balloons

Translation into another language is a derivative. Here the original is in German, translated into English. The first two versions were recorded by Nena in 1984. The Goldfinger version (as performed by John Feldman) combines both English and German and is covered by a §115 mechanical license.

---

99 Red Balloons

You and I in a little toy shop
Buy a bag of balloons with the money we've got
Set them free at the break of dawn
'til one by one, they were gone
Back at base, bugs in the software
Flash the message, something's out there
Floating in the summer sky
99 red balloons go by.

99 red balloons floating in the summer sky
Panic bells, it's red alert
There's something here from somewhere else
The war machine springs to life
Opens up one eager eye
Focusing it on the sky
As 99 red balloons go by.

99 decision street, 99 ministers meet
To worry, worry, super-scurry
Call out the troops now in a hurry
This is what we've waited for
This is it boys, this is war

The president is on the line
As 99 red balloons go by.

99 kriegsminister
Streichholz und benzinkanister
Hielten sich fuer schlaue leute
Witterten schon fette beute
Riefen: krieg und wollten macht
Mann, wer haette das gedacht
Dass es einmal soweit kommt
Wegen 99 luftballons
Wegen 99 luftballons

99 dreams I have had
In every one a red balloon
It's all over and I'm standing pretty
In the dust that was a city
If I could find a souvenir
Just to prove the world was here...
And here it is, a red balloon
I think of you and let it go.

◀   "99 Luftballons" – Nena (German)

◀   "99 Red Balloons" – Nena (English)

◀   "99 Red Balloons" – Goldfinger (English and German)

PROFIT IN DERIVATIVES

James Bond 007

Albert "Cubby" Broccoli

In the late 1950's, Mr. Broccoli and his partner, Harry Saltzman, bought the screen rights to the novels of Ian Fleming, and proceeded to make Mr. Fleming's character, James Bond, Agent 007, a household name. The 17 Bond films Mr. Broccoli produced during his lifetime were reported to have earned over $1 billion worldwide.

Sean Connery as James Bond (1963)

James Bond Films

1. *Dr. No* (1962)

2. *From Russia With Love* (1963)

3. *Goldfinger* (1964)

4. *Thunderball* (1965)

5. *You Only Live Twice* (1967)

6. *On Her Majesty's Secret Service* (1969)

7. *Diamonds Are Forever* (1971)

8. *Live and Let Die* (1973)

9. *The Man with the Golden Gun* (1974)

10. *The Spy Who Loved Me* (1977)

11. *Moonraker* (1979)

12. *For Your Eyes Only* (1981)

13. *Octopussy* (1983)

14. *A View to a Kill* (1985)

15. *The Living Daylights* (1987)

16. *License to Kill* (1989)

17. *GoldenEye* (1995)

18. *Tomorrow Never Dies* (1997)

19. *The World is Not Enough* (1999)

20. *Die Another Day* (2002)

21. *Casino Royale* (2006)

22. *Quantum of Solace* (2008)

Casino Royale

The only James Bond story for which Albert Broccoli never obtained the rights is *Casino Royale* which was first produced for American TV in 1954. Charles Feldman bought the rights to the book in the late 1950's, but never did anything with them.

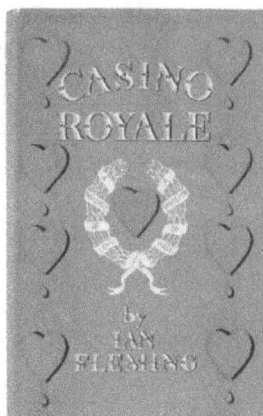

When Broccoli and Saltzman started making money with their Bond movies for United Artists in 1962, Feldman wanted to cash in with Columbia Pictures. In 1967 instead of making *Casino Royale* a "straight" movie, he chose to attempt a parody. Critics have called it *"a terrible, terrible movie, terrible, terrible, terrible... Casino Royale is a movie beyond salvation. It's one of Hollywood's greatest mistakes, a miserable catastrophe in every sense."* The best thing from the movie was the song "The Look of Love" which was an international hit.

◀   "The Look of Love" – Dusty Springfield

In the 1990s, Sony Pictures Entertainment (which had acquired Columbia Pictures) decided to make its own serious adaptation of *Casino Royale* and had also announced plans to produce its own rival Bond series. However these plans were laid to rest when Sony settled a legal action with MGM/UA in 1999 giving up any rights to the James Bond character.

After MGM's acquisition of the film rights to *Casino Royale* there was speculation that an official version would be produced. In 2004, a Sony/Comcast consortium acquired the Bond film series rights from co-owner United Artists. Soon after, in 2005, it was announced by EON Productions that their next James Bond adventure would in fact be *Casino Royale*.

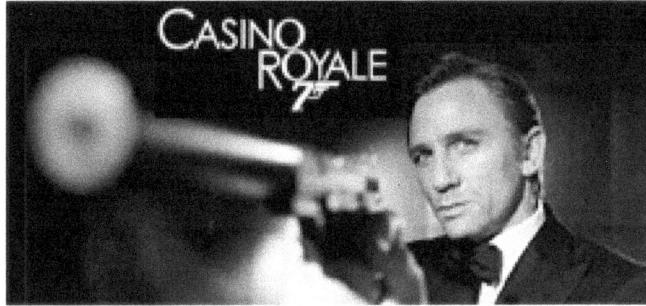

Daniel Craig as 007 in the 21st Bond film (2006)

To date, the Bond films have earned over $4 billion in box office receipts plus countless millions in home video.

MODULE 10: §115 MUSICAL EXAMPLES

The compulsory license established by §115 of the Copyright Act is a limitation on the exclusive rights granted to copyright holders under §106. To balance the competing interests of monopoly and free transmission of ideas, a cover of an original song is allowed. A §115 license to record a cover version only applies if the original composition was released on a U.S. phonorecord, and only for a cover version released on another U.S. phonorecord.

> **§101 Definition**
>
> "**Phonorecords**" are material objects in which sounds, other than those accompanying a motion picture or other audiovisual work, are fixed by any method now known or later developed, and from which the sounds can be perceived, reproduced, or otherwise communicated, either directly or with the aid of a machine or device. The term "phonorecords" includes the material object in which the sounds are first fixed.

Vinyl, cassette tapes, MP3s and CDs are phonorecords. Soundtracks in videos and DVDs are not, because they are audiovisual works. The compulsory license provided in §115 would not apply to those formats and a synchronization license from the music publisher is required.

Publishers must allow labels to make cover versions of previously recorded compositions. Nevertheless, they can veto sync, video, advertising, parody, sheet music, and other uses of the composition as in dramatic musical works, such as Broadway musicals and operas.

If your intent is to make a cover version of a non-dramatic composition previously released to the U.S. public on a phonorecord; then you may arrange the music to suit your style. The cover of the original cannot change the basic melody or character of the first work, for that would be creating a derivative. The cover version can be arranged differently as long as it preserves the basic melody.

As long as a label follows the guidelines of §115 and pays the statutory fee, then a music publisher can not prohibit a cover version.

ARRANGEMENTS

The right granted under §115 to create a new arrangement for a cover version in order to conform it to the style or manner of another artist's interpretation is difficult to grasp without examples.

Too much change makes it a derivative work, which is not allowed under the compulsory license. This would violate the exclusive §106(2) right to make a derivative, held by the copyright owner.

Musical Examples

Layla

Same author and performer, but re-arranged for MTV Unplugged. It changed from a power rock anthem to a more intimate ballad. All that was different was the arrangement, not the melody or fundamental character of the work, so a Section 115 license is applicable.

◀ "Layla" (original) – Derek and the Dominos

◀ "Layla" (MTV Unplugged) – Eric Clapton

I Will Always Love You

Originally performed by Dolly Parton is a country style, it was rearranged for Whitney Houston's R&B diva style. Both versions were hits. A §115 license is needed for Whitney Houston's record, but a synchronization license from the publisher is necessary for the movie. Remember that a compulsory license is only applicable to phonorecords, not audiovisual works.

◀ "I Will Always Love You" – Dolly Parton

◀ "I Will Always Love You" – Whitney Houston

My Way

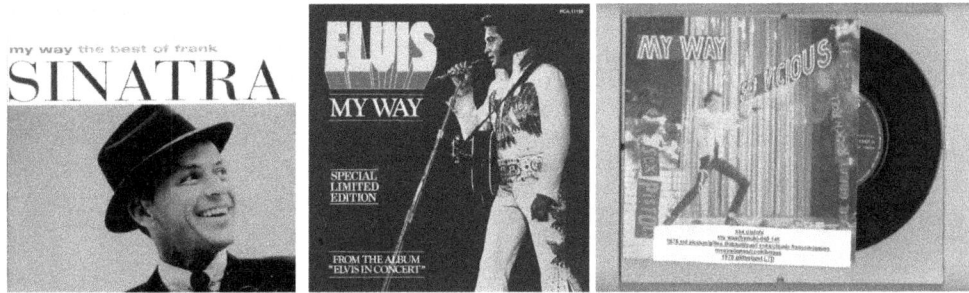

While on holiday in the south of France, Paul Anka heard the 1967 French pop song, "Comme d'habitude" with music by Jacques Revaux and lyrics by Gilles Thibault. He flew to Paris to negotiate the rights to the song. Back in New York, Anka re-wrote the original French song for Sinatra, subtly altering the melodic structure and changing the lyrics.

Frank Sinatra recorded his version of the song on December 30, 1968 and it was rush-released in early 1969. It reached #27 on the U.S. charts. On January 12, 1973 Presley performed the song during his show *Aloha from Hawaii* to a world-wide satellite television audience that topped one billion viewers.

The Sinatra and Elvis versions are standards. The Sex Pistols definitely arranged the tune in their own style; but the basic melody and fundamental character of the song are retained, therefore a §115 license is applicable.

◀   "My Way" 1969 – Frank Sinatra

◀   "My Way" 1973 – Elvis Presley

◀   "My Way" The Sex Pistols

The National Anthem

Faith Hill's performance uses a straightforward arrangement. Hendrix added sound effects for "the bombs bursting in air." However Jimi Hendrix did not need a §115 license to arrange a public domain work. Anyone can adapt and use a public domain work.

The performance of the anthem by an American Sign Language chorus is also a derivative translation into another language.

◀ "National Anthem" – Faith Hill

◀ "National Anthem" – Jimi Hendrix

Purple Haze

Cover versions can go both ways. Here, a psychedelic rock piece was arranged for a classical sting quartet. Same melody and fundamental character, therefore a §115 compulsory license is applicable.

◀ "Purple Haze" – Jimi Hendrix

◀ "Purple Haze" – Kronos Quartet

Mack The Knife

The Beggar's Opera was written by John Gay and opened in London in 1728. The play was a theatrical success and became the most popular play of that century. Its first season had an unprecedented run of sixty-two nights.

No adaptation has been more popular than Bertolt Brecht and Kurt Weill's *Die Dreigroschenoper (ThreePenny Opera)* first performed in post war Germany, in August 1928.

◀ "Die Moritat Von Mackie Messer" – Kurt Weill

Die Moritat von Mackie Messer

Und der Haifisch, der hat Zähne
und die trägt er im Gesicht
und Macheath, der hat ein Messer
doch das Messer sieht man nicht.

Ach, es sind des Haifischs Flossen
rot, wenn dieser Blut vergießt.
Mackie Messer trägt 'nen Handschuh
drauf man keine Untat liest.

An 'nem schönen blauen Sonntag
liegt ein toter Mann am Strand
und ein Mensch geht um die Ecke
den man Mackie Messer nennt.

Und Schmul Meier bleibt verschwunden
und so mancher reiche Mann
und sein Geld hat Mackie Messer
dem man nichts beweisen kann.

Jenny Towler ward gefunden
mit 'nem Messer in der Brust
und am Kai geht Mackie Messer
der von allem nichts gewußt.

Und das große Feuer in Soho
sieben Kinder und ein Greis -
in der Menge Mackie Messer, den
man nicht fragt und der nichts weiß.

Und die minderjährige Witwe
deren Namen jeder weiß
wachte auf und war geschändet -
Mackie, welches war dein Preis?
Wachte auf und war geschändet -
Mackie, welches war dein Preis?

Hildegard Knef's version only uses six verses of the eleven in the original "Die Moritat von Mackie Messer." Dick Hyman's is a simple instrumental.

🔊 "Mackie Messer" – Hildegard Knef

🔊 "Mack The Knife" – Instrumental Dick Hyman

Marc Blitzstein wrote an authorized English translation of the *Die Dreigroschenoper* in 1954. Blitzstien's adaptation opened off Broadway in 1955 and ran six years.

The Ballad of Mack the Knife – Blitzstein

Oh the shark has/ Pretty teeth dear
And he keeps them/ Pearly white
And a jackknife/ Has Macheath dear
and he keeps it/ Out of sight

When the shark bites/ with its teeth dear
Scarlet billows/ Start to spread
Fancy gloves though/
Wears Macheath dear
So there's not a trace of red

On the sidewalk/ Sunday morning
Lies a body/ Oozing life
Someone's sneaking/ Around the corner
Is that someone/ Mack the Knife?

There's a tugboat/ By the river
Cement bags/ Drooping down
The cement's/ Just for the weight dear
Now that Mackie's/ Back in town

Louie Miller/ Disappeared dear
After drawing/ Out his cash
And Macheath spends/ Like a sailor
Has our boy done/ Something rash?
Suki Tawdry, Jenny Diver, Lotte Lenya, Lucy Brown
The line forms/ On the right dear
Now that Mackie's/ Back in town

Louis Armstrong released his famous version of "Mack the Knife" in 1956. It charted at #20 in 1956. Bobby Darin's version was #1 for 9 weeks in 1959. Darin's only #1 song, it also won the Grammy for "Record of the Year" in 1959. Blitzstein needed permission to translate the work. Armstrong's and Darin's labels also needed permission to record the dramatic work as a popular tune.

◀ "Mack The Knife" – Louie Armstrong

◀ "Mack The Knife" – Bobby Darin

Light My Fire

This is one of the few songs to be in the Billboard top five twice with two different artists. The two most covered compositions are "Yesterday" and "White Christmas."

◀ "Light My Fire" – The Doors

◀ "Light My Fire" – Jose Feliciano

The Moral of The Story

Write hit songs. Encourage cover versions that sell millions of copies. Retire on your §115 mechanical license income.

MODULE 11: FORMALITIES AND REGISTRATION

HISTORY OF THE LIBRARY OF CONGRESS

The Library of Congress was established by an act of Congress in 1800 when President John Adams signed a bill providing for the transfer of the seat of government from Philadelphia to the new capital city of Washington. The legislation described a reference library for Congress only, containing "such books as may be necessary for the use of Congress - and for putting up a suitable apartment for containing them therein…"

Established with $5,000 appropriated by the legislation, the original library was housed in the new Capitol until August 1814, when invading British troops set fire to the Capitol Building, burning and pillaging the contents of the small library.

Recreation of Jefferson's library

Within a month, retired President Thomas Jefferson offered to sell his personal library to Congress at a price they could name. In this letter to his friend President James Madison, Jefferson seeks his support for the sale, which members of Congress were then debating.

The letter from Thomas Jefferson

…in the late events at Washington, I have felt so much for you that I cannot withhold the expression of my sympathies… Learning by the papers the loss of the Library of Congress, I have sent my catalogue to S.H. Smith, to make to their Library Committee the offer of my collection…

In January 1815, Congress accepted Jefferson's offer, appropriating $23,950 for his 6,487 books, and the foundation was laid for a great national library. Thomas Jefferson compiled this detailed list of books in his library after agreeing to sell his collection to Congress.

Jefferson noted books missing from his collection, as well as those added after his catalog had been completed. Jefferson paid particular attention to the size of the books because that was the basis upon which the purchase price was calculated.

Jefferson's inventory

The Library of Congress and the Copyright Office

Today's Library of Congress is an unparalleled world resource. The collection of more than 130 million items includes more than 30 million cataloged books and other print materials in 460 languages; more than 58 million manuscripts; the largest rare book collection in North America; and the world's largest collection of legal materials, films, maps, sheet music, and sound recordings.

The secret to the growth of the Library is simple. Since 1870, the law requires that copies of works be sent to the Library of Congress and its Copyright Office as mandatory deposits to accompany applications for copyright registration.

FUNCTIONS OF THE COPYRIGHT OFFICE

The Constitution gave Congress the power to enact laws establishing a system of copyright in the United States. Congress enacted the first Federal copyright law in May 1790, and the first work was registered within two weeks. Originally, claims were recorded by Clerks of U.S. District Courts.

Not until 1870 were copyright functions centralized in the Library of Congress under the direction of the Librarian of Congress, Ainsworth Rand Spofford. The Copyright Office became a separate department of the Library of Congress in 1897, and Thorvald Solberg was appointed the first Register of Copyrights.

1897 copyright deposits as they were waiting to be sorted, counted, and classified

The Copyright Office is the place where claims to copyright are registered and where documents relating to copyright may be recorded. The Copyright Office registers over 600,000 claims to copyright each year. Since its start, it has recorded over 30,000,000 registrations.

Receiving and Processing Division

This Division receives all incoming mail and records and deposits payments for copyright fees; creates automated in-process records for all claims and fees received; routes registrations; maintains files; assigns copyright registration numbers; and creates and mails certificates of registration.

Examining Division

The Examining Division examines all applications, copies, phonorecords, and other material presented to the Copyright Office for the registration of copyright claims to determine their acceptability. It resolves errors, omissions, and inconsistencies in claims and develops policies and practices to administer the copyright law and provide guidance to examiners and the public.

Cataloging Division

The Cataloging Division records the descriptions and the copyright facts of all works registered in the Copyright Office, thus providing reference access to all information of record relating to registrations, deposits, assignments, and other documents.

Information and Reference Division

This Division responds to all copyright information and reference requests from the public; produces and supplies Copyright Office forms and publications; furnishes search reports based on Copyright Office records; and prepares certifications and other legal documents.

Licensing Division

The Licensing Division is in charge of administering compulsory and statutory licenses. The Division collects royalty fees from cable operators for retransmitting television and radio broadcasts; from satellite carriers for retransmitting "super-station" and network signals; and from importers or manufacturers who distribute digital audio recording devices or media in the United States.

Copyright Acquisitions Division

The Copyright Acquisitions Division is responsible for using and enforcing the mandatory deposit requirement of the Copyright Act of 1976 and Copyright Office regulations to acquire works needed for the collections of the Library of Congress.

WHY REGISTER?

Copyright protection starts the moment the work is created in fixed form. The copyright in the work of authorship immediately becomes the property of the author who created the work. Only the author or those deriving their rights through the author can rightfully claim copyright. There are several excellent reasons to register a claim to copyright.

- Registrations are public records identifying the copyright claimant;

- Registration is necessary before an infringement suit can be filed in court;

- Registration is *prima facie* evidence in court of a claim to ownership;

- If registration is made within three (3) months after publication or before an infringement, the claimant may ask for statutory damages and attorney's fees;

- Registration is necessary to obtain certain compulsory royalties; and

- Registration protects against the importation of infringing copies of the registered work.

POOR MAN'S COPYRIGHT

Obtaining copyright protection by mailing your work to yourself and not opening the envelope is an urban myth. Although it may have a postmark showing the date of mailing, it is not a substitute for registration. It's a waste of time and money because it has no legal benefits for infringement lawsuits. It will still be necessary to file for registration of a claim in the Copyright Office before a lawsuit. The postmarked envelope is not a public record or solid proof in court. Why do you think they call it the *"poor man's copyright?"*

WHO FILES THE REGISTRATION FORM?

Only the following persons are legally entitled to file:

- The author;

- The copyright claimant;

- The employer if the work was made for hire;

- The owner of one or more of the exclusive right(s); and/or

- A duly authorized agent of the above persons.

EFFECTIVE DATE OF REGISTRATION

A registration may be filed at any time within the life of the copyright. Registration is effective on the date the Copyright Office receives all the required elements in acceptable form, regardless of how long it takes to process the application and mail the certificate of registration. The Copyright Office gets over 600,000 applications a year; so the time the Copyright Office requires to process an application may take several months.

If registration is made within three (3) months after the first publication of the work, the effective date of protection is retroactive to the date of publication. A registration filed prior to an infringement of the work gives the copyright owner the option for asking for either actual or statutory infringement penalties.

CREATION DATE AND PUBLICATION DATE

The date of creation is not the same as the date of publication. All works have a date of creation, some works have also been published.

---

§101 Definition

A work is "**created**" when it is fixed in a copy or phonorecord for the first time.

"**Publication**" is the distribution of copies or phonorecords of a work to the public by sale or other transfer of ownership, or by rental, lease, or lending. The offering to distribute copies or phonorecords to a group of persons for purposes of further distribution, public performance, or public display constitutes publication. A public performance or display of a work does not of itself constitute publication.

In the case of works for hire, anonymous, and pseudonymous works, the creation date and publication date are essential for calculating the duration of copyright protection.

---

§302 Duration of copyright: Works created on or after January 1, 1978

(c) Anonymous Works, Pseudonymous Works, and Works Made for Hire.—In the case of an anonymous work, a pseudonymous work, or a work made for hire, the copyright endures for a term of 95 years from the year of its first publication, or a term of 120 years from the year of its creation, whichever expires first.

NOTICE

The use of a copyright notice is no longer required under U.S. law; although it is important because it informs the public that the work is protected by copyright, identifies the copyright owner, and shows the year of first publication. The © notice is used only on visually perceptible copies. If a work is infringed, and a proper notice of copyright appears on the published copy, then no defense based on innocent infringement is possible. Innocent infringement occurs when the infringer did not realize that the work was protected.

The notice should contain all the following three elements:

- The symbol © (the letter C in a circle), or the word "Copyright," or the abbreviation "Copr."

- The year of first publication of the work

- The name of the owner of copyright in the work

        Example: © 2000 Wolfgang A. Mozart

The notice for phonorecords embodying a sound recording should contain all of the following three elements:

- The symbol ℗ (the letter P in a circle)

- The year of first publication of the sound recording

- The name of the owner of copyright in the sound recording

    Example: ℗ 2000 RCA Records Inc.

REGISTRATION FORMS

Most registrations will use one of these forms:

Form PA: If the work could be performed in front of an audience, use this form. Categories include musical works and lyrics, dramatic works, and plays (including accompanying music), pantomimes, dance, motion pictures, videos, and other audiovisual works. Use the same form whether or not the work has been published (offered for sale to the public).

Form SR: Use this for published and unpublished sound recordings. These are works that result from the recording of musical, spoken, or other sounds, like special effects or bird calls. Form SR protects the sound recording, not the underlying composition. Use Form PA if you want to register a movie soundtrack or the audio part of a filmstrip, because these are considered part of an audiovisual work as a whole.

Form TX: Use this form for published and unpublished non-dramatic literary works. Form TX is appropriate for written items like novels, short stories, poetry, essays, textbooks, nonfiction books, catalogues, compilations of information, databases, and computer programs. If the work is part of a newspaper, magazine, periodical, or serial, use Form SE.

Form SE: Use this form for published works that are parts of a newspaper, magazine, periodical, or serial.

Form VA: Pictorial, graphic, 2-dimensional, and sculptural works, including architectural works (published and unpublished) are registered using this form. Some of the items registered on this form include paintings, drawings, graphics, applied art, photographs, prints, art reproductions, maps, globes, charts, technical drawings, diagrams, and models.

In 2009 paper versions of these forms were superseded by Form CO, an online registration procedure. Although paper forms are still accepted, online registration is less costly.

REGISTRATION FORM CHECKLIST

Every copyright registration form asks for the same basic information in the same spaces.

Space 1	What is the title of the work?
	Does it have another title?
	What is the nature of the work?

Space 2	Who created it?
	Was it a work-for-hire?
	Is it a joint work?
	How many authors contributed?
	What are their real names?
	When were they born?
	Are they still alive? If not, when did they die?
	Are they U.S. citizens?
	Did they use their real or pen names?
	What did each one contribute to the work?

Space 3	When was it completed?
	Was it released for sale? When? Where?

Space 4	Who is claiming ownership in the copyright?
	If it's not the author, what is the basis of their claim?
	Was there an Assignment of Copyright?
	Was a work-for-hire agreement signed before creation?

Space 5	Was this work registered before?
	If so, why is another registration needed?
	What is the previous registration number and date?

Space 6   Is this a derivative work or compilation?
            What was the preexisting material? What was added?

Space 7   Who should the Copyright Office contact for additional information?

Space 8   Who is signing and submitting the form?
            If it is not the author, what authority do they have?

Space 9   Where is the certificate going to be mailed?

ⓘ   Library of Congress   http://www.loc.gov/

ⓘ   Copyright Office   http://www.copyright.gov/

ⓘ   Online Copyright registration http://www.copyright.gov/eco/

MODULE 12: MUSIC PUBLISHING

THE ESSENCE OF THE DEAL

A songwriter transfers his copyright to a music publisher in exchange for the publisher's promise to pay a portion of income to the writer. Of course, there is no such thing as a "standard publishing deal." There may be several writers with varying percentages of joint ownerships, or more than one publisher. However, in all cases, the duties and responsibilities of the parties are similar.

DUTIES OF THE PUBLISHER

Protect the Work

As an owner of exclusive rights in the work, the publisher has the authority to sue infringers of the work on its own behalf, and on behalf of the writers and others who have a beneficial interest in the work. The publisher files the Form CO or Form PA registration at the Copyright Office.

Exploit the Work

Since the music publisher holds the copyright by assignment from the author, or authors, the publisher has all the §106 rights. The publisher exploits the rights granted by law, and turns those exclusive rights into money for the publisher and the writers.

A publisher is essentially a sales agent for the tune. It is in the best interests of both parties for the publisher to actively "work" the song, and get it on a record, or in a movie or TV show. An unlicensed composition does not earn any income, so there is no money for the publisher or writer. Most publishing contracts require that sheet music copies or a recording of the composition be made before a deadline, or the copyright reverts to the authors.

§106(1) and (3) Make and Distribute Copies

This is the most basic function of the publisher. The original job of the publisher was to engrave, print, and sell sheet music copies of the author's composition. Before records and movies, this was the main way to earn income from a song.

Under the §115 mechanical license, the publisher earns fees from record labels for copies of the composition, made not with ink and paper, but on phonorecords (CD, vinyl, cassettes), and by digital downloads of sound recordings of performances of the composition.

§106(2) Derivatives

As owner of the exclusive right to make derivatives, the publisher authorizes all derivative uses of the song such as translations, parodies, commercial uses, and arrangements.

The right to make a derivative use of a composition by putting it in timed relation with visual images is called the synchronization or *sync right*. Uses of a song in a movie or television program are not covered by the §115 compulsory license, so the publisher is free to negotiate any sync fee he chooses. Essentially the publisher has an absolute veto over any derivative use of the work. Non-approved derivatives are infringements of the copyright.

§106(4) and (5) Public Performance and Display

As the owner of the right to public performance of the work, the publisher "clears" the song through ASCAP, BMI, or SESAC. After a recording has been released to the public, the publisher registers that composition with a performing rights organization so it is eligible to earn fees from broadcast and other public performances.

Collect and Distribute Income

There are several sources of music publishing income:

- Radio and TV broadcast performances ASCAP, BMI, and SESAC
- Live concert and night club performances ASCAP, BMI, and SESAC
- §115 mechanical license fees 9.10¢ per copy of the composition
- Negotiated synchronization licenses for movies and TV
- Advertising, commercial, and parody uses of the composition
- Sales of sheet music copies and lyric reprint rights
- Ring tones, digital downloads

- Toys, video games, novelty items, and other special uses
- Grand rights (dramatic rights) for stage productions

Sub-Publishers

Because the §106 rights granted under law are recognized worldwide, U.S. publishers may hire sub-publishers to administer and collect royalties earned by the composition in foreign territories. For example, a U.S. publisher may grant all §106 rights to a foreign sub-publisher, but only for one country.

In order to maximize income, a publisher may grant an exclusive sub-publishing right to a specialty publisher. For example, a publisher may grant §106(1)(3) exclusive print rights to a sub-publisher that specializes in sheet music folios.

FOUR BASIC TYPES OF PUBLISHING CONTRACTS

- Standard (*Straight*)
- Co-Publishing (*Co-Pub*)
- Administration (*Admin*)
- Sub-Publishing (*Sub-Pub*)

Different answers to these questions distinguish the four types of publishing contracts:

- Who owns the copyright?
- If there is more than one owner of the copyright, what percentage does each own?
- What are the obligations of the publisher to the writer?
- What are the obligations of the publisher to other publishers?
- Are all or only part of the rights being transferred?
- Is the contract limited to a certain territory?
- If the song earns a dollar, how much does everyone get paid?
- How long does the contract last? A few years? Life of the copyright?
- Do the copyrights revert to another party?
- Can the parties terminate the deal?

Standard Publishing Deal

Composers transfer 100% of copyright to a publisher in exchange for the publisher's promise to pay 50% of income to the writers. This deal is usually for the life of the copyright, but the authors (or their heirs) still retain the 35 year termination right.

Co-Publishing Deal

- Two or more publishers own the copyright (often an equal split)
- One of the publishing companies may be owned by the songwriter
- The two co-publishers pay the author a total of 50% of the song's income

Administration Deal

An administrating publisher collects and distributes income from the song, but does not own the copyright. The administrator takes a fee and remits the balance to the publisher who then pays the songwriter according to the publishing contract. Ownership of the copyright never changes hands in an administration deal.

Sub-Publishing

The publisher who owns the copyright grants an exclusive right and/or an exclusive territory to another publisher.

EXAMPLES OF OWNERSHIP AND CASH FLOW

Joint Authorship Equals Joint Ownership

Three authors, Tom, Dick and Harry co-write a song. They each own an undivided 33.3% of the copyright. Since they have not assigned their copyright, to a publishing company they act as their own publishers. Any of the owners can license the song as long as they account and pay their co-owners, and not destroy the song's value. They each receive 1/3 of the income earned by the song.

Writers :

100 %	Copyright Ownership
100 %	Earnings

If the song earns $1.00 the 3 owners receive:

Tom	$ 0.333
Dick	$ 0.333

Harry	$ 0.333
Total	$ 1.00

Straight Publishing Deal

Tom, Dick and Harry then enter into a publishing deal, and assign 100% of their copyright to a publishing company. The publisher agrees to pay them ½ of the money it receives.

Writers :		Publisher :	
0 %	Copyright Ownership	100 %	
50 ¢	Earnings	50 ¢	

The Publisher receives $1.00 from use of the song and pays the writers 50¢:

Tom	$ 0.166		
Dick	$ 0.166		
Harry	$ 0.166		
Total	$ 0.50	Publisher keeps	$ 0.50

Beneficial Interest

Harry dies. His widow Betty inherits Harry's right to receive royalties, also called a **beneficial interest**. She doesn't inherit the copyright because her husband already signed his 1/3 over to the publisher. There is no change in the ownership of the copyright, just a change in who gets Harry's share of income as 1/3 writer.

Writers :		Publisher :	
0 %	Copyright Ownership	100 %	
50 ¢	Earnings	50 ¢	

The Publisher receives $1.00 from use of the song and pays as follows :

Tom	$ 0.166		
Dick	$ 0.166		
Betty	$ 0.166	(as the beneficial interest in George's share)	
Total	$ 0.50	Publisher keeps	$ 0.50

Betty inherited the beneficial interest in 1/3 of the writers' share of income which equals 1/6 of the total income ($ 0.166 of each dollar).

Co-Publishing Deal

Amanda creates her own publishing company (named Solo Publishing). She assigns 100% of her copyright to it in exchange for ½ of the royalties earned by the song and received by Solo Publishing. Since she is both the composer who is assigning the work, and the owner of the publishing company, she will sign the contract in both of her capacities.

Solo Publishing then enters a co-publishing deal with Major Publishing Co. and splits the copyright ownership (and gross income) 50% − 50%.

Writer :		Publisher :
0 %	Copyright Ownership	50% Major Publishing Co. and 50% Solo Publishing
50 ¢	Earnings	50 ¢

Major Publishing Co. receives $1.00 from use of the song and pays half of its income to Solo and keeps the other half :

Solo Publisher	$ 0.50
Major Publisher	$ 0.50
Total	$ 1.00

However Solo and Major still have to pay ½ of their gross income to Amanda as the writer. The final net distribution of $1.00 earned by the song :

Solo pays Amanda	$ 0.25	Solo keeps	$ 0.25
Major pays Amanda	$ 0.25	Major keeps	$ 0.25
Writer's Total	$ 0.50	Publishers' Total	$ 0.50

Amanda earns 50¢ as the writer of the song, and since she owns Solo, her publishing company earns 25¢.

Administration Deal

Tiny Publishing Co. owns the copyright to a song through a standard publishing deal with a writer. Tiny doesn't have the resources to administer the copyright; so it signs an administration deal with a larger company. The administrator gets 10% of the total song income as a fee, but does not own any part of the copyright.

Writers :		Publisher :
0 %	Copyright Ownership	100 % Tiny Publishing
		0 % Administrator
50 ¢	Earnings	50 ¢

The Administrator receives $1.00 from use of the song and pays as follows :

Administrator	$ 0.10	kept as a administration fee
Tiny Publishing	$ 0.90	net earnings after fee
Total	$ 1.00	

Tiny Publishing still has to pay the writer ½ of its income under the standard publishing deal. Distribution of $1.00 earned by the song :

Administrator	$ 0.10
Tiny Publishing	$ 0.45
Writer	$ 0.45
Total	$ 1.00

Conclusion

Publishing is the heart of the music business. Like a fertile field that is well-managed by a farmer; a single hit song can generate enough income to support a songwriter for the rest of his life and the lives of his children. The highest compliment that can be paid to composers is to say "They live off their royalties."

MODULE 13: INFRINGEMENT

FREE TRANSMISSION OF IDEAS VERSUS MONOPOLY

The Copyright Act reflects the balancing of the historical tension between monopoly and the free transmission of ideas. The law clearly lists the rights granted to authors and owners, and outlines the limits on those rights.

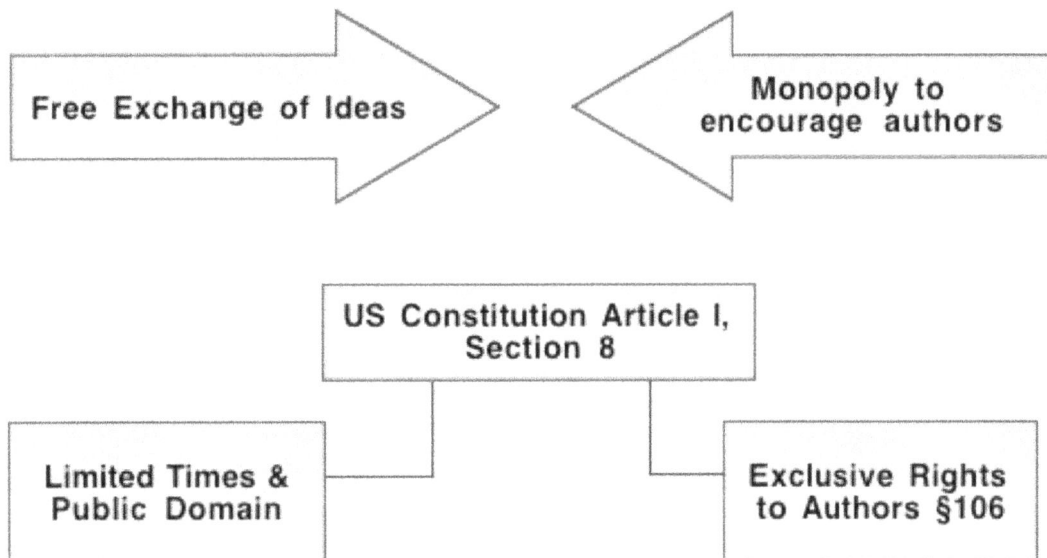

Free Exchange of Ideas

Monopoly to encourage authors

US Constitution Article I, Section 8

Limited Times & Public Domain

Exclusive Rights to Authors §106

EXCLUSIVE RIGHTS

Title 17 of the U.S. Code (The Copyright Act) puts the Constitution into effect by giving authors and owners certain exclusive (monopoly) rights in their works.

---

§106 Exclusive Rights

Subject to sections 107 through 122, the owner of copyright under this title has the exclusive rights to do and to authorize any of the following:

(1) to reproduce the copyrighted work in copies or phonorecords;

(2) to prepare derivative works based upon the copyrighted work;

(3) to distribute copies or phonorecords of the copyrighted work to the public by sale or other transfer of ownership, or by rental, lease, or lending;

(4) in the case of literary, musical, dramatic, and choreographic works, pantomimes, and motion pictures and other audiovisual works, to perform the copyrighted work publicly;

(5) in the case of literary, musical, dramatic, and choreographic works, pantomimes, and pictorial, graphic, or sculptural works, including the individual images of a motion picture or other audiovisual work, to display the copyrighted work publicly; and

(6) in the case of sound recordings, to perform the copyrighted work publicly by means of a digital audio transmission.

LIMITATIONS ON EXCLUSIVE RIGHTS

In order to balance the tension between the owner's monopoly and the free transmission of ideas, the Copyright Act places many restrictions on their exclusive rights. Sections 107 through §122 limit the exclusive rights granted in §106.

§107   Fair use

§108   Reproduction by libraries and archives

§109   Effect of transfer of a particular copy or phonorecord (First Sale Doctrine)

§110   Exemption of certain performances and displays (The TEACH Act)

§111   Secondary transmissions (cable TV)

§112   Ephemeral recordings (transient copies made in the course of broadcasting)

§113   Scope of exclusive rights in pictorial, graphic, and sculptural works (Reproduction in or on any kind of article, whether useful or otherwise, example: building murals)

§114   Scope of exclusive rights in sound recordings (Excludes any right of performance under §106(4) for Form SR ℗ copyrights.)

§115	Compulsory license for making and distributing phonorecords (Mechanical Licenses)
§116	Negotiated licenses for public performances by jukeboxes
§117	Computer programs (backup copies)
§118	Noncommercial broadcasting licensing agreements (PBS and NPR)
§119	Secondary transmissions of super-stations and network stations for private home viewing
§120	Scope of exclusive rights in architectural works (Pictorial representations permitted, alterations to, and destruction of buildings by owners permitted)
§121	Reproduction for blind or other people with disabilities
§122	Secondary transmissions by satellite carriers within local markets

§501 INFRINGEMENT

The definition of infringement is simple and straightforward. Any use of a copyrighted work without the permission of the owner or as permitted in §107 through §122 is an infringement of copyright.

---

§501 Infringement of copyright

(a) Anyone who violates any of the exclusive rights of the copyright owner as provided by sections 106 through 122… is an infringer of the copyright.

(b) The legal or beneficial owner of an exclusive right under a copyright is entitled… to institute an action for any infringement of that particular right committed while he or she is the owner of it.

Direct Infringement

This term applies to the actual person or business that commits the infringement. Their actions directly violate §106. There has been an unauthorized use or unauthorized copying of a work protected by copyright.

Contributory Infringement

If a person or business materially contributes to or aids the infringing conduct of another person, they can be held liable for contributory infringement. In short, their knowledge and participation in another's infringement exposes them to the same penalties as the direct infringer.

An analogy comes from criminal law. A getaway driver is just as guilty of a crime as a bank robber. The driver knew what the bank robber was doing, helped him evade the police, and benefited from the crime.

Vicarious Infringement

Vicarious liability can be imposed on a person or business that controls or supervises the activity of an infringer and receives a direct financial benefit from the infringement. The responsibility of the employer is to supervise the activities of an employee. A record store that "looks the other way" while its employees sell bootleg CDs can't evade liability by pleading ignorance.

REGISTRATION

Although copyright protection begins the moment an author fixes his original expression in tangible form; registration of the author's claim to ownership is recommended. Registering a claim to copyright creates a public record of ownership and must be filed before any infringement suit can be filed in court.

Registration also counts as *prima facie* evidence of the truth of the information contained on the registration forms. This means that instead of requiring the author to prove ownership, the burden shifts to the infringer to disprove the author's claim of ownership.

If a work is registered within 3 months of its first publication, or before an infringement takes place, the owner can also ask for statutory damages and attorney's fees.

PROVING INFRINGEMENT

There are four required elements to prove infringement:

- Ownership of a valid copyright

- Illicit use of an exclusive right by copying or other unauthorized action

- Access to the original work by the defendant

- Substantial similarity between the original and infringing works

1	OWNERSHIP of a VALID COPYRIGHT

2	COPYING or UNAUTHORIZED USE

3	ACCESS

4	SUBSTANTIAL SIMILARITY

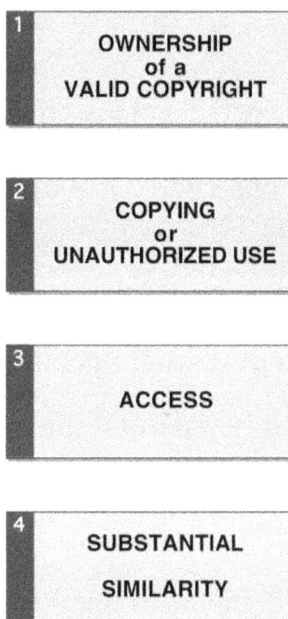

Valid Copyright

Only the owner of the copyright, or the legal or beneficial holder of an exclusive right can sue infringers. For example, if a song was infringed, the music publishing company (as owner of the copyright), the author (as beneficial owner) or a licensee (as holder of an exclusive right) could file the lawsuit.

All infringement lawsuits are federal cases because copyright protection is granted under Title 17 of the U.S. Code. If the registration was filed within five years of the first publication of the work; the court will presume that the plaintiff owns a valid copyright without need of further proof.

Copying or Unauthorized Use

There is no infringement of a work unless it has been copied or used without permission. It is infringement if illicit copies of the work were made or if a portion of the original was incorporated into another work.

Access

If there is no access by the infringer to the original work, copying is impossible. Sometimes the access is direct, but most often access must be proven circumstantially. Perhaps the original work was widely performed on radio and TV, or sold thousands of sheet music copies. The more widely the work was distributed, the more likely the infringer had access to the original.

Substantial Similarity

This is the most difficult thing to prove in an infringement case. There is no clear rule defining what makes an infringing work substantially similar to the original. Courts approach this issue as an "ordinary observer." It is up to a jury composed of average citizens, not expert musicologists to determine the similarity of works.

The similarities must be of the original expressions of the author. A copy of a short musical phrase may not meet the substantial similarity test, because that short phrase may not be original enough to warrant copyright protection in itself.

There is no rule permitting the use of a minimum amount of another author's work. This misconception (the 8 note rule, the 4 bar rule, etc.) is not a rule at all. Even two notes may be enough to convince an ordinary observer. For example, think of the two notes from the theme to the movie *Jaws*.

The more an infringing work is similar to the original, the more likely the infringer had access to the original. Mere coincidence could explain only some resemblances, not all.

EXAMPLES

No Valid Copyright: Boogie Chillen–La Grange

In 1948, John Lee Hooker and Bernard Besman wrote a musical composition called "Boogie Chillen." A recording of the song was released later that year and eventually up to one million copies were sold. Later, Hooker assigned his rights in the composition to Besman, who registered "Boogie Chillen" with the Copyright Office in 1967.

ZZ Top released their song "La Grange" in 1973. Since then, the song has had global circulation as a phonorecord, has been featured in prominent national television advertising, and has been performed at thousands of concerts.

Besman learned about "La Grange" in 1991 and filed an infringement suit against ZZ Top, Billy Gibbons, Dusty Hill, Frank Beard, and their publisher, Hamstein Music Company.

The court ruled that under the Copyright Act of 1909, musical compositions entered the public domain 28 years after recordings were first sold to the public. Thus the 1948 release, whose registration was never renewed, had entered the public domain in 1976. The 1991 infringement suit was 15 years too late, as the copyright had expired.

🔊 "Boogie Chillen" – John Lee Hooker

🔊 "La Grange" – ZZ Top

Subconscious Copying: He's So Fine–My Sweet Lord

The Chiffons   **George Harrison**

"He's So Fine" was recorded by the Chiffons in 1962 and became a number one hit. The court concluded that due to its popularity, Harrison had access to the song and subconsciously copied the melody.

The judge explained "…Did Harrison deliberately use the music of 'He's So Fine?' I do not believe he did so deliberately. Nevertheless, it is clear that 'My Sweet Lord' is the very same song with different words, and Harrison had access to 'He's So Fine.' This is, under the law, infringement of copyright, and is no less so even though subconsciously accomplished…"

🔊 "He's So Fine" – The Chiffons

🔊 "My Sweet Lord" – George Harrison

Double Infringement: Super Freak–(U) Can't Touch This

Rick James

MC Hammer

This is an interesting case of two infringements in one. The first infringement was of the composition, that is, the Form PA ©. The melody was appropriated and the lyrics were changed by MC Hammer. The second infringement of the Form SR ℗ was committed when the sound recording was sampled and used in the MC Hammer record. Both Rick James' publishing company (Jobete Music Co.) and Motown records had infringement claims against MC Hammer, his label (Capitol Records) and publisher (Stone City Music).

◄   "Super Freak" – Rick James

◄   "(U) Can't Touch This" – MC Hammer

The Ordinary Observer Test: Kanon–Hook–Graduation

Pachelbel

Popper

Vitamin C

Decide this one for yourself. Because Pachelbel's *Kanon und Gigue in D-Dur* (*Canon in D Major*) is in public domain, anyone can make alterations and derivatives. Did John Popper use one of the best known melodies from 1680 to make a point in his ironic song "Hook?" You be the judge.

When you listen to the two samples, keep in mind the chord progression [I V vi iii IV I IV V]. Isn't the chord progression the "hook" that's made the *Kanon* memorable for over 300 years? If you don't think Hook is based on the *Kanon*, listen to "Graduation (Friends Forever)" by Vitamin C.

The basso ostinato from the Kanon

🔊 *Kanon und Gigue in D-Dur*

🔊 "Hook" – The Blues Travelers

🔊 "Graduation (Friends Forever)" – Vitamin C

HOOK by John Popper

A   E   F#m C#
It doesn't matter what I say

D   A   D   E
So long as I sing with inflection

A   E   F#m C#
That makes you feel that I'll convey

D   A   D   E
Some inner truth of vast reflection

A   E   F#m C#
But I've said nothing so far

D   A   D   E
And I can keep it up as long as it takes

A   E   F#m C#
And it don't matter who you are

D   A   D   E
If I'm doing my job then it's your resolve that breaks

A   E   F#m C#
Because the hook brings you back

D   A   D   E
I ain't tellin' you no lie

A   E   F#m C#
The hook brings you back

D   A   D   E
On that you can rely

There is something amiss
I am being insincere
In fact I don't mean any of this
Still my confession draws you near
To confess the issue I refer
To familiar heroes from long ago
No matter how much Peter loved her
What made the Pan refuse to grow

Was that the hook brings you back
I ain't tellin' you no lie
The hook brings you back
On that you can rely

--Harmonica Solo--

Suck it in suck it in suck it in
If you're Rin Tin-Tin or Anne Boleyn
Make a desperate move or else you'll win
And then begin
To see
What you're doing to me this MTV is not for free
It's so PC it's killing me
So desperately I'll sing to thee
Of love
Sure but also rage and hate and pain and fear of self
And I can't keep these feelings on the shelf
I've tried well no in fact I've lied
Could be financial suicide but I've got too much pride inside
To hide or slide
I'll do as I decide and let it ride until I've died
And only then shall I abide this tide
Of catchy little tunes
Of hip three minute ditties
I wanna bust all your balloons
I wanna burn all of your cities
To the ground I've found

I will not mess around
Unless I play then hey
I will go on all day hear what I say
I have a prayer to pray
That's really all this was
And when I'm feeling stuck and need a buck
I don't rely on luck because...

The hook brings you back
I ain't tellin' you no lie
The hook brings you back
On that you can rely

Conclusion

It's never easy to prove infringement, each occurrence must be examined on a case-by-case basis. All four elements of infringement must be present and blatant enough to convince an ordinary observer that the exclusive rights granted to authors and owners under §106 were violated.

MODULE 14: REMEDIES AND DAMAGES

What makes copyright infringement an issue of major importance in the entertainment industry is the severity of its penalties. The penalties provided under the Copyright Act of 1976 fall into three categories: Criminal, Physical, and Money Damages.

CRIMINAL PENALTIES

Congress has always preferred that individual copyright owners pursue civil remedies, that is, owners suing infringers for money damages in court. However, in certain egregious circumstances criminal penalties are warranted, especially for counterfeit labeling, pirating phonorecords, making bootlegs of live performances, and other "willful" infringements.

**CRIMINAL COPYRIGHT
INFRINGEMENT PENALTIES**

18 U.S.C. §2318

Counterfeit labels

up to 5 years

§506

Fraudulent © Notice

$2,500 fine

18 U.S.C. §2319

Record Piracy

up to 10 years

18 U.S.C. §2319a

Bootlegging

up to 5 years

PHYSICAL REMEDIES

In both criminal and civil cases, a federal judge has the power to put an immediate stop to the manufacture and distribution of infringing copies. In rare cases, the court may impose this injunction even before a trial. If a plaintiff wins an infringement suit, part of the judgment will include a permanent injunction preventing the defendant from the future manufacture and distribution of infringing copies.

Sometimes simply ordering a defendant to stop producing illegal copies is not enough. The court can demand that the infringing copies, along with all master tapes and matrices required for manufacturing be seized and held, thus preventing their use to manufacture more copies. Furthermore, the judge can order the destruction of those copies and masters.

**PHYSICAL COPYRIGHT INFRINGEMENT
PENALTIES**

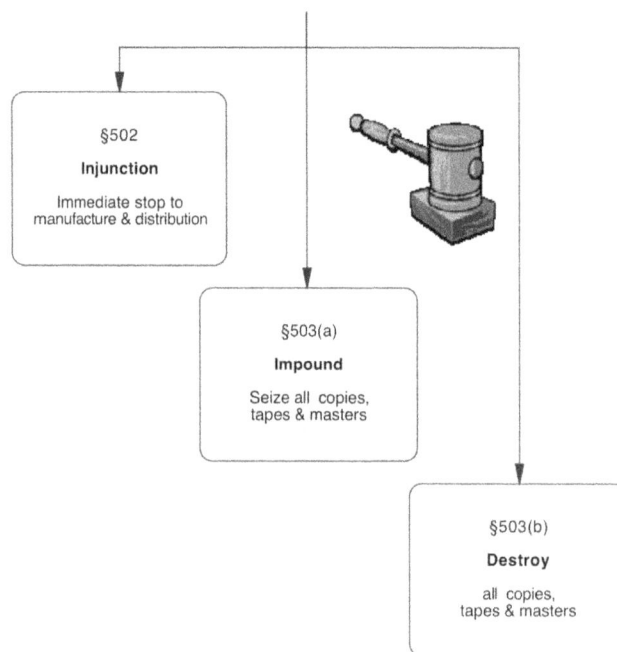

§502

Injunction

Immediate stop to
manufacture & distribution

§503(a)

Impound

Seize all copies,
tapes & masters

§503(b)

Destroy

all copies,
tapes & masters

MONEY DAMAGES: A CHOICE OF REMEDIES

Most infringement cases are civil lawsuits, meaning that the owner of a valid copyright sues an infringer in court for money, an injunction, and destruction of the offending copies. Although the copyright in a work exists from the moment of fixation of the original expression of an author, registration of a claim to copyright is required before commencing an infringement suit. [Title 17 U.S. Code §411]

If a copyright claimant filed a registration before infringement, (or within 3 months of the first publication of the work), then the plaintiff (owner) has the choice of asking for either the actual damages suffered due to the infringement, or statutory damages. In either case, if the registration preceded the infringement, the owner can also request that the infringer pay his attorneys' fees and all costs of the litigation. [Title 17 U.S. Code §412]

> **§504 Remedies for infringement: Damages and profits**
>
> (a) In General. Except as otherwise provided by this title, an infringer of copyright is liable for either:
>
> (1) the copyright owner's actual damages and any additional profits of the infringer, as provided by subsection (b); or
>
> (2) statutory damages...

MONEY DAMAGES

a choice

§504(b) **Actual Damages**	**OR**	§504(c) **Statutory Damages**

§505 **Costs of Suit & Attorney's Fees**

The Copyright Owner <u>may choose</u> between Actual **or** Statutory Damages

ONLY IF THE COPYRIGHT WAS REGISTERED BEFORE THE INFRINGEMENT
(or within 3 months of 1st publication)

ACTUAL DAMAGES §504(B)

If no registration was filed before infringement, the copyright owner is limited to asking for actual damages plus the profits made by the infringer. For actual damages, a publisher might only receive the same amount he would have gotten under if he issued a license for his work.

On the other hand, the publisher might also argue that the infringed composition was the hit song that drove the sales of the defendant's platinum album. If this is the case, the label's profits are connected to the infringement, a portion of which will be awarded to the plaintiff.

---

§504(b) Actual Damages and Profits

The copyright owner is entitled to recover the **actual damages** suffered by him or her as a result of the infringement, **and any profits of the infringer** that are attributable to the infringement and are not taken into account in computing the actual damages. In establishing the infringer's profits, the copyright owner is required to present proof only of the infringer's gross revenue, and the infringer is required to prove his or her deductible expenses and the elements of profit attributable to factors other than the copyrighted work.

---

§504(b) ACTUAL DAMAGES

**Recover the actual
damages suffered**

+

**The profit made by the
infringer**

STATUTORY DAMAGES §504(C)

Unlike actual damages, statutory damages allow for a range of possible sums to compensate the plaintiff whose work was infringed. An owner has the choice of asking for either actual or statutory damages only if the registration was filed before the infringement, or within 3 months of first publication of the work.

Under statutory damages, is not necessary to actually prove the actual dollar amount of the economic injury suffered by the copyright owner.

---

§504(c) Statutory Damages

(1) Except as provided by clause (2) of this subsection, the copyright owner may elect, at any time before final judgment is rendered, to recover, instead of actual damages and profits, an award of statutory damages for all infringements involved in the action, with respect to any one work, for which any one infringer is liable individually, or for which any two or more infringers are liable jointly and severally, in a sum of not less than **$750** or more than **$30,000** as the court considers just. For the purposes of this subsection, all the parts of a compilation or derivative work constitute one work.

---

(2) In a case where the copyright owner sustains the burden of proving, and the court finds, that infringement was committed **willfully**, the court in its discretion may increase the award of statutory damages to a sum of not more than **$150,000**. In a case where the infringer sustains the burden of proving, and the court finds, that such infringer was not aware and had no reason to believe that his or her acts constituted an infringement of copyright, the court in its discretion may reduce the award of statutory damages to a sum of not less than **$200**.

§504(c) STATUTORY DAMAGES

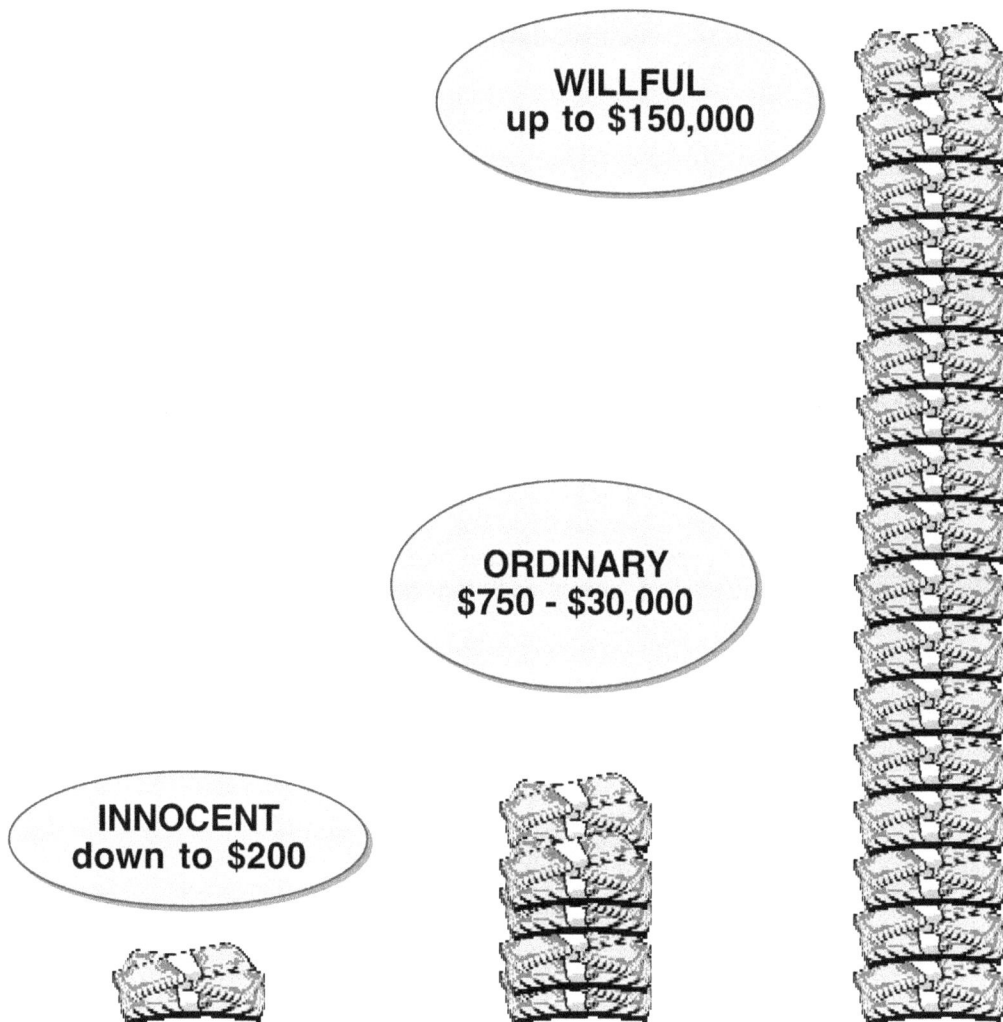

**WILLFUL
up to $150,000**

**ORDINARY
$750 - $30,000**

**INNOCENT
down to $200**

"Ordinary" damages range from $750 to $30,000. Of course, the original author would argue that the defendant's actions were willful; and ask for the highest possible amount of statutory damages: $150,000.

The defendant would argue that he was not aware and no reason to believe that he infringed the work, thus his infringement was merely "innocent." If the defendant can prove so the amount he pays to the plaintiff might be reduced to $200.

ATTORNEY'S FEES AND COSTS §505

An incentive for registering your copyright is the ability to ask for reimbursement of attorney's fees and costs expended in the infringement suit.

---

§505 Remedies for infringement – Costs and attorney's fees

In any civil action under this title, the court in its discretion may allow the recovery of full costs by or against any party... the court may also award a reasonable attorney's fee to the prevailing party as part of the costs.

The important thing to remember here is that an owner who registers the work upon publication (or within 3 months of 1st publication), has many more options if the work is infringed. It is easier to persuade an attorney to take your infringement suit if there is a possibility that the infringer will be forced to pay legal fees.

---

§412 Registration as prerequisite to certain remedies for infringement

In any action under this title, ...no award of statutory damages or of attorney's fees, as provided by sections 504 and 505, shall be made for —

(2) any infringement of copyright commenced after first publication of the work and before the effective date of its registration, unless such registration is made within three months after the first publication of the work.

MODULE 15: DEFENSES AND FAIR USE

DEFENSES TO COPYRIGHT INFRINGEMENT

Defenses to a complaint of copyright infringement are used at the trial of the infringer. The accused infringer will try to break the chain of the four questions the owner must prove – Ownership of a valid copyright, Copying (or unauthorized use), Access, and Substantial Similarity.

OWNERSHIP

Only the author or owner of exclusive rights in a work may sue for copyright infringement. The plaintiff must first prove that he owns the copyright in the original work. Registration of an owner's claim to copyright is only *prima facie* evidence; the defendant can attack it. A defendant may prove that the work was not written by the plaintiff, or that there was no valid license or transfer of ownership to him.

COPYRIGHTABILITY

Not Original

Defendants regularly challenge the originality of a prior work to undermine the validity of its copyright. If the plaintiff's work is not original, then he has no basis for his own copyright, therefore he cannot sue infringers.

Not Fixed

A work must be fixed for it to be copyrightable. The original author must submit a deposit copy to the Copyright Office with his registration form. A court will compare the plaintiff's deposit copy against the work accused of infringing the original.

Not the Expression of an Idea

In order to have a valid copyright, an author must create an original expression of an idea. Myriad authors may express the same idea in as many ways. Protection is attached to the original expression of the idea. An idea itself is free for all to use.

PUBLIC DOMAIN

Every year there are many well-known songs, novels, pictures, and literary works which have reached the end of the limited term of copyright protection. When a work falls into public domain it loses the protections of §106, and anyone is free to copy it or make derivatives. The Constitution grants protection for limited times, after that time has passed, the interests of the public's access to the work outweighs the author's monopoly.

For works first published before 1978, the complete absence of a copyright notice from a published copy generally indicates that the work is not protected by copyright. Sound recordings were not copyrightable in the U.S. before February 15, 1972.

STATUTE OF LIMITATIONS

The law allows a copyright owner up to three years from the date of an infringement to sue. Even if the work had been infringed for the previous 10 years, only profits earned by the infringer within three years prior to filing suit can be recovered as actual damages.

ABANDONMENT OF COPYRIGHT

A copyright owner can voluntarily relinquish any or all of his exclusive §106 rights. This intent to abandon must be clearly stated, not implied from the owner's inaction against other infringers. The most common example of copyright abandonment is computer shareware where the author of the program allows users to freely copy and distribute the software. The owner has abandoned his rights, so he cannot later sue users for infringement.

Creative Commons provides a license that affirmatively places the work in the public domain with no §106 rights reserved for the author.

INDEPENDENT CREATION

Since the requirement of a fixed original expression is all that is necessary to create a copyrightable work, it is uncommon, but not impossible for two authors to express the same idea in similar ways. If one author has no access to the other's work, copying is impossible, even though the works may be substantially similar.

Both Isaac Newton (1643–1727) and the German mathematician Gottfried Leibniz (1646–1716) developed calculus independently and nearly simultaneously. Since neither had access to the other's work, this a classic case of independent creation.

DE MINIMUS COPYING

If only a small amount of the prior work is taken, how substantially similar can the two works be?

FRAUD ON THE COPYRIGHT OFFICE

The fine print at the bottom of a registration form warns that anyone who knowingly makes a false representation of a material fact is subject both to a fine and the loss of his claim to a copyright in that work.

MISUSE OF COPYRIGHT

This is a very rare defense. It may be argued that a copyright is being used to further censorship or an illegal purpose. For example, this defense has been contemplated in a case where the Church of Scientology sued prior members for publishing its religious texts.

INNOCENT INTENT IS NOT A DEFENSE

Enough said.

DEFENSES TO INFRINGEMENT

> **Use of exclusive rights without permission is Infringement**

Plaintiff is not the Owner (no valid ©)	Independent Creation (no access)
Not Copyrightable (no valid ©)	De minimus copying (not substantial)
Public Domain (© protection ended)	Fraud on the Copyright Office
3 Year Statute of Limitations (§507)	Misuse of ©
Abandonment (no §106 rights)	Fair Use (§107)

THE FAIR USE DEFENSE

Copyright is a balancing act between encouraging authors by creating exclusive rights, and favoring the free transmission of ideas by limiting those rights. Section 106 of the Copyright Act grants exclusive rights to authors. Section 107 limits those exclusive rights in favor of the free transmission of knowledge.

The principle of "Fair Use" is perhaps the most misunderstood aspect of copyright law. Fair use is not permission to do what you want, but a defense in court after you have already been sued for copyright infringement.

> **§107 Limitations on exclusive rights: Fair use**
>
> Notwithstanding the provisions of sections 106 and 106A, the fair use of a copyrighted work... for purposes such as criticism, comment, news reporting, teaching, scholarship, or research, is not an infringement of copyright.
>
> In determining whether the use made of a work in any particular case is a fair use the factors to be considered shall include—
>
> (1) the purpose and character of the use, including whether such use is of a commercial nature or is for nonprofit educational purposes;

(2) the nature of the copyrighted work;

(3) the amount and substantiality of the portion used in relation to the copyrighted work as a whole; and

(4) the effect of the use upon the potential market for or value of the copyrighted work.

Four Factors of Fair Use

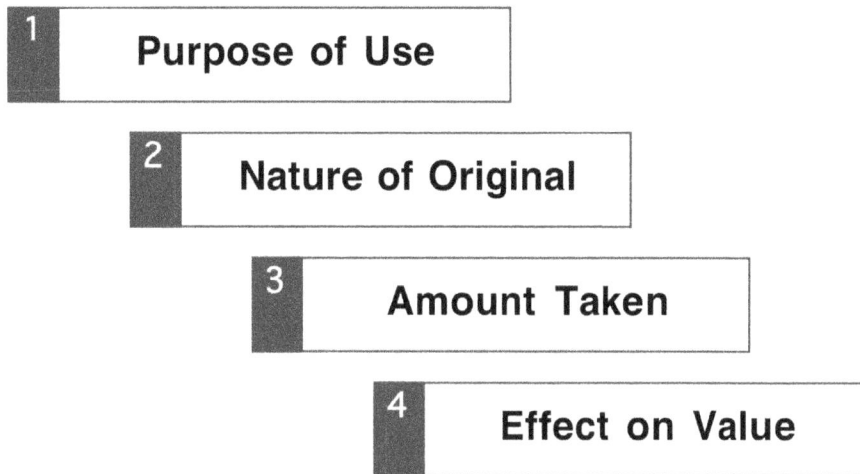

1 **Purpose of Use**

2 **Nature of Original**

3 **Amount Taken**

4 **Effect on Value**

FOUR FACTORS

The easiest way to analyze a possible fair use is to break down the four factors and list the pros and cons. No single factor is more important than the others. Courts look to all the factors before deciding that an unauthorized use falls under the protection of §107. A determination of Fair Use requires analysis of these aspects of the Four Factors:

Purpose of Use

Favoring Fair Use	Opposing Fair Use
Teaching	Commercial activity
Research/Scholarship	Entertainment

Non-profit institution	For-profit corporation
Criticism/Comment/News	Verbatim replay only
Original transformed to new use	Mere reiteration of original
Access restricted to students	Wide audience
Parody of the original	Broad parody beyond original

Nature of the Original Work

Favoring Fair Use	Opposing Fair Use
Published	Original work unpublished
Non-fiction/factual	Fiction

Amount Taken

Favoring Fair Use	Opposing Fair Use
Small amount used	Substantial portion taken
Non-essential parts used	Unique elements taken

Effect on Market for Original Work

Favoring Fair Use	Opposing Fair Use
No lost sales	Substitute for purchase
No effect on value of original	Destroys value of original
Limited copies made	Multiple copies made
One time use	Unlimited potential re-use

Fair use is not a right – it's an excuse.

CAMPBELL V. ACUFF-ROSE MUSIC, INC.

The protection of parody as a form of Fair Use was addressed in the "Pretty Woman" case. Luther Campbell, lead singer of the band 2 Live Crew wanted to re-record the famous Roy Orbison song and add his own satirical lyrics. Campbell's label requested a license from Orbison's music publisher Acuff-Rose, and was denied.

Campbell proceeded with his version anyway. Acuff-Rose sued, claiming Campbell's version was an unauthorized derivative thus infringing its §106(2) rights. Campbell's position was that he was commenting on the original song, and thus protected under the Fair Use exemption.

The Supreme Court examined the four §107 factors, and came to this conclusion as stated by Justice Kennedy in his concurring opinion:

> "...certain general principles are now discernable to define the fair use exception for parody. One of these rules is that **parody may qualify as fair use** regardless of whether it is published or performed for profit. Another is that parody may qualify as fair use **only if it draws upon the original composition to make humorous or ironic commentary about that same composition.** It is not enough that the parody uses the original in a humorous fashion, however creative that humor may be. The parody must target the original, and not just its general style, the genre of art to which it belongs, or society as a whole..."

Campbell v. Acuff-Rose Music, Inc., 510 U.S. 569 (1994)

This is a very fine line. Campbell could parody "Pretty Woman" by commenting on the girl in the song, but Fair Use does not allow him to change the lyrics to comment on something else.

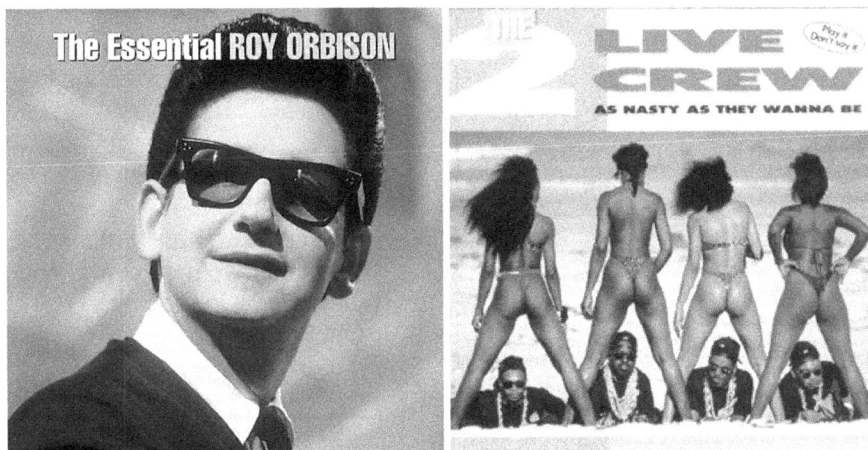

◀ "Oh, Pretty Woman" (Orbison & Dees)

◀ "Pretty Woman" (Campbell)

Oh, Pretty Woman
by Roy Orbison and William Dees

Pretty Woman, walking down the street,
Pretty Woman, the kind I like to meet,
Pretty Woman, I don't believe you, you're not the truth,
No one could look as good as you

Mercy

Pretty Woman, won't you pardon me,
Pretty Woman, I couldn't help but see,
Pretty Woman, that you look as lovely as can be
Are you lonely just like me?

Pretty Woman, stop a while,
Pretty Woman, talk a while,
Pretty Woman, give your smile to me,

Pretty Woman, yeah, yeah, yeah
Pretty Woman, look my way,
Pretty Woman, say you'll stay with me
'Cause I need you, I'll treat you right, Come to me baby, Be mine tonight

Pretty Woman, don't walk on by,
Pretty Woman, don't make me cry,
Pretty Woman, don't walk away, Hey, O.K.
If that's the way it must be, O.K., I guess I'll go home now it's late
There'll be tomorrow night, but wait!

What do I see
Is she walking back to me?
Yeah, she's walking back to me!
Oh, Pretty Woman

Pretty Woman
by Luther Campbell

Pretty Woman, walking down the street,
Pretty Woman, girl you look so sweet,
Pretty Woman, you bring me down to that knee,
Pretty Woman, you make me wanna beg please,

Oh, Pretty Woman

Big hairy woman, you need to shave that stuff,
Big hairy woman, you know I bet it's tough
Big hairy woman, all that hair ain't legit,
Cause you look like Cousin It

Big hairy woman

Bald headed woman, girl your hair won't grow,
Bald headed woman, you got a teeny weeny afro
Bald headed woman, you know your hair could look nice,
Bald headed woman, first you got to roll it with rice

Bald headed woman here, let me get this hunk of biz for ya,
Ya know what I'm saying, you look better than Rice a Roni

Oh, Bald headed woman

Big hairy woman, come on in,
And don't forget your bald headed friend
Hey Pretty Woman, let the boys
Jump in

Two timin' woman, girl you know it ain't right,
Two timin' woman, you's out with my boy last night
Two timin' woman, that takes a load off my mind,
Two timin' woman, now I know the baby ain't mine
Oh, Two timin' woman
Oh, Pretty Woman.

Weird Al

"Weird Al" Yankovic has made a career of recording parody versions of popular songs. In fact, some songwriters think that have truly "made it" when one of their compositions is parodied. The music publisher holding the copyright in the song is glad to issue a *parody license* for a derivative that will generate additional income. A §115 license is not applicable because the lyrics and intent of the song are changed even though the melody remains the same. A parody license may or may not be granted by the publisher at whatever rate he chooses.

No matter what Coolio says, Weird Al's label got the music publisher's permission to parody "Gangsta's Paradise." No record label would expose themselves to a claim of willful infringement. The song's owner holds the §106(2) derivative rights, not Coolio. If he did not want his work parodied, he should have negotiated that clause in his publishing agreement. Nevertheless, Coolio will earn income as co-writer of the melody and original lyrics.

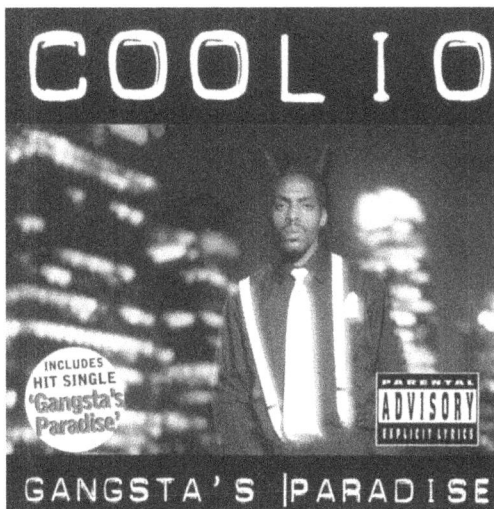

◀   "Gangsta's Paradise" – Coolio

◀   "Amish Paradise" – Yankovic

MODULE 16: RECORDING CONTRACTS

THE INDUSTRY

Record companies are in the business of recording and selling musical performances. They own and exploit all the §106 rights in the Form SR ℗ sound recording of an artist's performance.

A label advances money to its recording artist to make sound recordings. The artist repays this "loan" from his share of sales. Bankers would call this a non-recourse loan; which means that the label can only get repaid by the sale or lease of the master tapes [§106(1) and (3)], or digital audio transmissions of the sound recordings [§106(6)]. If nobody buys the album, the artist does not have to sell his house or car to repay the advances.

The record industry is one of the riskiest businesses in the world, even riskier than oil drilling or betting at the race track. Only five percent (5%) of all records released in the U.S. earn enough for the artist to recoup the recording costs and his advance.

Next Year's Hits

Nobody knows what is going to be popular in the future, but some musician is in the studio right now recording what will be the biggest hit of next year, or the biggest flop of next year. Since there is no guarantee that anyone will even buy the record, a label has to limit its risks.

You cannot be in the record business with only one recording. Labels have to make sure that a hit record pays for itself and for all the failures (>95%) and still earns enough money to record more artists. They do this several ways by keeping costs low and trying to make everything recoupable from an artist's royalties.

Essence of the Deal

An artist is specially commissioned by a label to make sound recordings of his performances. The label pays the costs of the recording, and advances money to the artist. The artist must repay these advances and recording costs out of his royalty percentage of sales income.

Deal Memo

A short deal memo highlights the main points of the negotiation between the artist's attorney and the legal affairs department of the label. The details are fleshed out later in the full contract.

There is no such thing as a "standard record deal." The question that must be asked is – who has the leverage in negotiations? A new unsigned act has no influence to bargain for a better royalty rate or a higher advance. A platinum selling act can re-negotiate an old deal with its new-found clout.

ANALYSIS OF A RECORDING CONTRACT

This is a paragraph-by-paragraph explanation of the sample contract for this module.

1. Parties, Territory, Term

The label is signing the musical group, and each member of the group; jointly, individually and in any combination as employees-for-hire. Even if a group member leaves, the ex-member is still under contract. Any new replacement member must agree to the same contract as the original band.

Examples: The Beatles, John and/or Paul and/or George and/or Ringo

The Commodores & Lionel Ritchie

Black Sabbath & Ozzy Osbourne

Destiny's Child & Beyoncé

The Police & Sting

Black Eyed Peas & Fergie

No Doubt & Gwen Stefani

The territory is usually stated as broadly as possible. Contracts used to call for a world-wide territory, but within the life of the copyright the sound recording may be sold in outer space.

Time is not calculated by the calendar in a recording contract. It is calculated by "contract periods" defined by the delivery of recorded masters.

2. Recording Procedure

The label, who is paying for the recording, will decide when and where the studio sessions take place. They also must approve the producer and the selection of songs to be recorded. A budget will be developed and agreed on that will estimate the studio time, equipment, and services needed to finish the production.

Delivery equals *fixation*. For copyright purposes it is the date of *creation*. Labels have the right to accept or reject the finished recordings.

There is no objective standard for a commercially acceptable recording. Labels may insist that the album contain no dirty words etc. If so, there has been no *delivery* (as defined by the contract), and the artist must re-record the tracks. A technically acceptable recording is the highest quality recording mixed down to the label's specifications, along with all outtakes or alternative takes, work mixes, and unused tracks. Everything recorded at the session, (including outtakes and alternate versions) belongs to the label as a work–for–hire.

All paperwork must be delivered too. This includes the entire J-card or jewel case copy, liner notes, a list of all cuts, timing, writers, publishers, sample clearances, American Federation of Musicians paperwork for union musicians, and immigration papers; in short everything. Album artwork, including photographs and graphics, is often considered a part of delivery.

3. Royalties

At signing, the label will pay artists an advance against their future royalties. Just as recording costs are recoupable, the advance is recoupable against an artist's percentage of sales. The **U.S. Base Royalty Rate** is the most important figure in the contract. All calculations for the rest of the contract are derived from this figure. To arrive at the **Gross Artist Royalty** in dollars, multiply the applicable royalty rate by the **Suggested Retail List Price** (SRLP) multiplied by the number of units sold. A good manager or attorney reviewing a recording contract will calculate the "penny rate," to determine exactly how much the artist gets paid for each record sold in each format.

The producer is a contract employee of the artist whose job it is to supervise the rehearsal, recording, and mixing sessions. The producer is paid either a salary, a fixed fee, or cash as advance against a producer's royalty.

All-in	As is the case in the sample contract, the producer's royalty is part of the artist's royalty. If the artist's U.S. base royalty rate is 13%, and the producer gets a 2% royalty, then the artist's net royalty is 11%.
Override	Producer's royalty is separate from artist's royalty.

The U.S. Base Royalty is usually increased for future option albums. This is an incentive the label is willing to give the artist. Major labels often adjust the U.S. Base Royalty Rate for different formats (CD, cassette, vinyl, new media) and for different retail prices (budget line, mid-line, record club, PX)

The U.S. Base Royalty Rate escalates (*Bumps*) upon the album reaching certain sales targets of gold (500,000 units) and platinum (1,000,000 units). Some contracts also reward top 40 chart position by increasing the artist's royalty. On the other hand, royalties are reduced for Canadian, European, and foreign releases.

Royalties for compilations are calculated as a fraction of the royalty rate for the number of artist's masters divided by the total number of masters on the album. For example if an artist recorded 5 of 12 masters on an album, multiply that fraction times the base royalty rate to determine the artist's royalty rate on the compilation:

U.S. Base Royalty Rate * 5/12 = Compilation Album Royalty Rate

---

A similar calculation is used when there is more than one royalty artist performing on the album.

4. Royalty Accounting

This clause sets out the mechanics of reporting royalties every 6 months. The label will only play the artist if his account is in a recouped position, meaning that the advances and recording costs have been repaid. The artist is allowed to audit the company's books and object to any miscalculations.

The most important thing to know about this section is the definition of *Recoupable Expenses*. Briefly, everything spent to create the sound recording is recoupable against the artist's account.

Always recoupable	Advances, studio costs, blank tape, engineers, sidemen, equipment rental, hotel, food, travel (to and from the studio session), union payments, payments to 3rd parties, sample usage licensing fees, artwork, graphics, photographs for the album, re-mixing fees, etc.
Recoupable if in contract	Tour support, independent promotion
Never recoupable	The label's pressing costs, distribution expenses, office overhead, shipping, office salaries

Records are considered *sold* when payment has been received by the label. However, often a substantial number of unsold records are subsequently returned to the label by retailers. To prevent the possibility of the label overpaying the artist for records that are later returned, a portion of the royalties due are set aside and paid to the artist (liquidated) in the next accounting periods.

Cross-Collateralization is the accounting technique whereby an artist's royalties from the sales of one album are used to recoup against all of the artist's other albums. If sales of some albums do not recoup recording costs, sales of a hit record go to recoup outstanding recording costs from their other releases first before the artist gets a check.

Cut-Outs are records sold for scrap or at less than 50% of wholesale price. You will find them in the bargain bin at the record store with the corner cut off or a hole drilled through the UPC code. Cut-outs earn no royalties for the artist.

Free Goods are also non-royalty bearing promotional or bonus copies for record reviewers, radio stations, DJ's, and others. Often a label will ship extra copies to retailers as an inducement to stock the record.

Example: Retailer receives 115 CDs but pays label for sales of only 100.

Retailer keeps the sales of the 15 free CDs as an incentive.

Packaging Deductions (Container Charges) are reductions in the U.S. Base Royalty Rate depending on the format of the album's release: CD, cassette, or vinyl. Even though these charges do not reflect current manufacturing costs, they are usually not negotiable. The label's argument is that they sell the sound recording, and that the artist should pay for any fancy packaging.

5. Exclusivity and Re-Recording Restriction

The artist is offering his personal services to record exclusively for the label for the term of the contract plus the re-recording restriction. This clause protects the label from an artist re-doing his hit for another label which would cut into the sales of the first release.

6. Copyrights

This clause makes the recording contract a work–for–hire. Thus the label is the owner of the Form SR ℗ copyright for 120 years from creation or 95 years from release to the public (whichever is shorter). Since the label owns the Form SR ℗ copyright, it has the §106 rights to the sound recording. If for some reason the contract is not considered a work–for–hire, then the artist assigns all rights he might have in the masters to the label.

7. Marketing

The label holds the perpetual and exclusive rights to manufacture records and/or license masters in all forms of use; including, but not limited to vinyl, CD, tapes, electronic transmission, CD-ROM, DVD, video games, digital downloads, streaming, or anything else that may be invented in the future. The label can exploit the sound recordings forever, even after the Form SR ℗ expires, as long as it accounts and pays to artist, or his heirs.

The label can sell the sound recordings under any trademark or label name, and at any price point: Top–Line, Mid–Line or Budget.

The label does not have to release the album. There is no "guaranteed release commitment" clause in most record contracts. For the purpose of marketing the album, the group grants the use of their names and likenesses to the label for advertising.

8. Warranties

The artist confirms that he is not under contract to another label, that no rights were previously granted to third parties, and that he will indemnify the label in case of a lawsuit.

9. Mechanical Licenses

The **Controlled Composition** clause applies when the recording artist has written, owns, or has an income or beneficial interest in a composition which he has recorded for the album.

Since these publishing payments to the recording artist-songwriter are not recoupable, the label is willing to pay only 75% of the statutory rate for the mechanical license. In addition, the total amount paid is usually capped at 10 * ¾ of statutory rate for the "short song" formula.

If the label pays the full mechanical royalty rate for all compositions on an album:

> **9.1¢ statutory rate * 12 compositions = $1.09 payable to publishers per album**

If the label uses a controlled composition clause plus 10 song cap, it saves 41¢ per CD in mechanicals for the label:

> **9.1¢ statutory rate * ¾ * 10 composition cap = 68¼¢ payable to publishers per album**

10. Lease of Masters

Under §106(3) the label has the right to authorize others to make and distribute copies of the master recordings. It is very common for a label to press and release CDs in the US, but to license that right to foreign companies for international sales. In that case, the only expense the label incurs is the duplication of the master recordings for the licensee.

11. Renewal Options

The sample contract is not a 6 record deal, but a 1 + 1 + 1 + 1 + 1 + 1 deal. Options to renew or **pick up** the contract for another album are always the choice of the label, never the artist. This arrangement gives a label the chance to opt-out of the contract. Another way this sample contract could be structured is to have a **two album firm** deal with four options; which would be a 2 + 1 + 1 + 1 + 1 deal. This guarantees that the artist will record at least two albums under the contract.

The renewal clause is a source of tension between artists and labels. A label wants the artist under contract for as long as possible, hoping that they have signed another Elvis or the Beatles. Since an artist has only one career, the artist wants as much flexibility as possible in the future.

Option periods are not defined by time passing, but by delivery of masters to the label within certain time frames. A label will sign an act, record, and release the first album, then wait to see sales results before picking up the option for another contract period.

12. Assignment

Record labels get bought and sold regularly, so the contracts with their recording artists must be freely assignable to a new owner.

13. Suspension

This clause puts the contract on hold if an artist does not fulfill his commitment. An artist cannot just wait out the contract period and refuse to record.

14. Definitions

Every word that is capitalized in a contract has a special meaning listed here.

15. Entire Agreement

Lawyers always put a clause similar to this in contracts. It states that no matter what someone may have said, if it is not in the contract, it doesn't count. Oral agreements are not worth the paper they are not printed on.

MODULE 17: RECORD ROYALTIES

THE MAGIC FORMULA

The most important concept to know about record royalties is contained in a simple formula. Negotiators are lost without a clear idea of all the variables that can change the computation.

A change in any of the three factors will affect the *penny rate*, or exactly how much in dollars and cents a sale will generate for the artist.

First multiply the U.S. Base Royalty Rate times the Suggested Retail List Price (SRLP) times the number of units sold. This will yield a dollar amount which is the Gross Artist Royalty Before Recoupment.

From this total, subtractions for container charges, recoupable recording costs, pre-paid advances against future royalties, and other deductions are made.

The net amount after repaying these expenses goes to the recording artist.

The Magic Formula

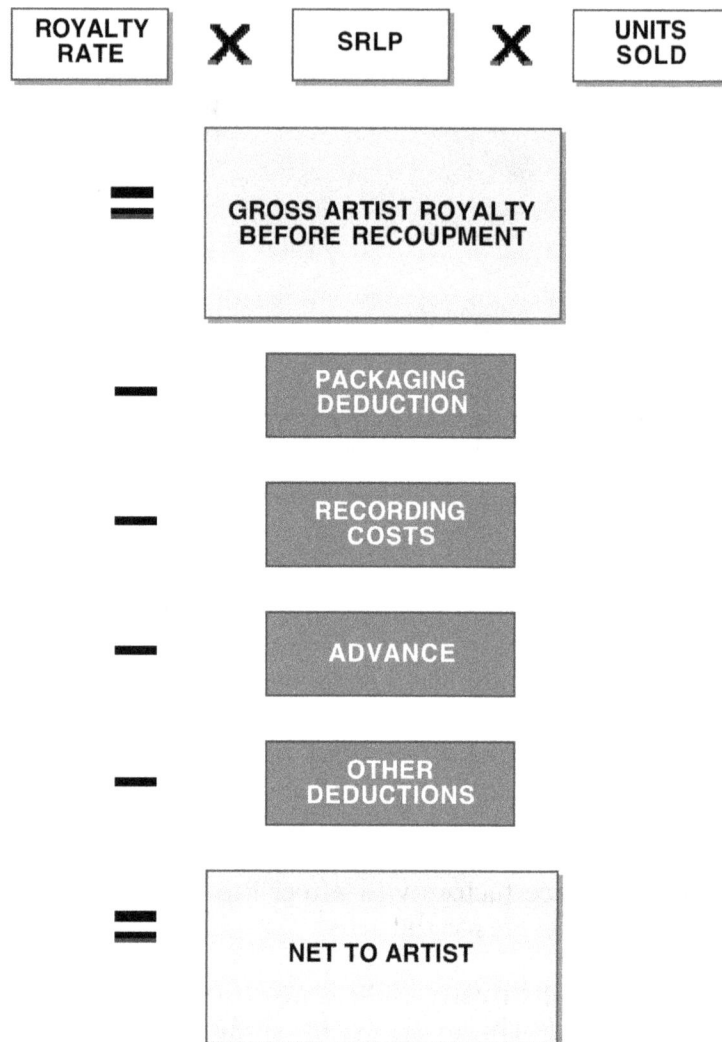

ROYALTY RATE	X	SRLP	X	UNITS SOLD

= GROSS ARTIST ROYALTY BEFORE RECOUPMENT

− PACKAGING DEDUCTION

− RECORDING COSTS

− ADVANCE

− OTHER DEDUCTIONS

= NET TO ARTIST

CHANGES IN ROYALTY RATES

With this formula, *only three variables can change*, the U.S. base royalty rate, the list price, and the number of units sold. A change in any one of the three affects the Gross Artist Royalty Before Recoupment. Managers and artists must look to the recording contract to determine the factors that may increase or decrease the royalty rate payable per unit sold.

Packaging deductions (container charges) are another way labels cut royalty rates. Artist royalties also vary depending on price points and formats. In a producer *all-in deal*, the producer's royalty is taken from the artist's royalty.

Changes in Royalty Rates

INCREASES IN ROYALTY RATES :

· ACHIEVING SALES GOAL

· ACHIEVING CHART POSITION GOAL

· NEXT ALBUM IN CONTRACT

DECREASES IN ROYALTY RATES :

· FOREIGN SALES

· LOWER PRICE POINT (mid-line, budget)

· DIFFERENT FORMATS (LP, cassette)

· SPECIAL MARKETS (Record Clubs, PX)

· PACKAGING DEDUCTIONS

· PRODUCER ALL-IN DEAL

· FREE GOODS (0% royalty)

· CUT-OUTS (0% royalty)

CHANGES IN SRLP

The second aspect that can vary in the equation is the Suggested Retail List Price (SRLP) of the album. In addition to a cut in the applicable contract royalty rate, a lower SRLP must be factored into the calculation.

Top–Line Record   retails for 100% of top-line SRLP (full price)

Mid–Line Record   retails from 68% to 85% of top-line SRLP

Budget Record   retails for less than 67% of top-line SRLP

The SRLP assumes that units are sold in *Normal Retail Channels*, meaning U.S. retail stores. Sales through mail order, PX, record clubs, discounters, and in foreign countries cut the artist's base royalty rate.

CHANGES IN UNITS SOLD

The record contract usually has a definition of what constitutes a *unit sold* which may differ by format. The artist must be aware that many units distributed to stores are promotional *free goods* and will not count as records sold. *Cut-outs* (sold at less than 50% of wholesale) are non-royalty bearing units. Labels often withhold royalty payments to artists in anticipation of the return of unsold units.

RECOUPABLE EXPENSES

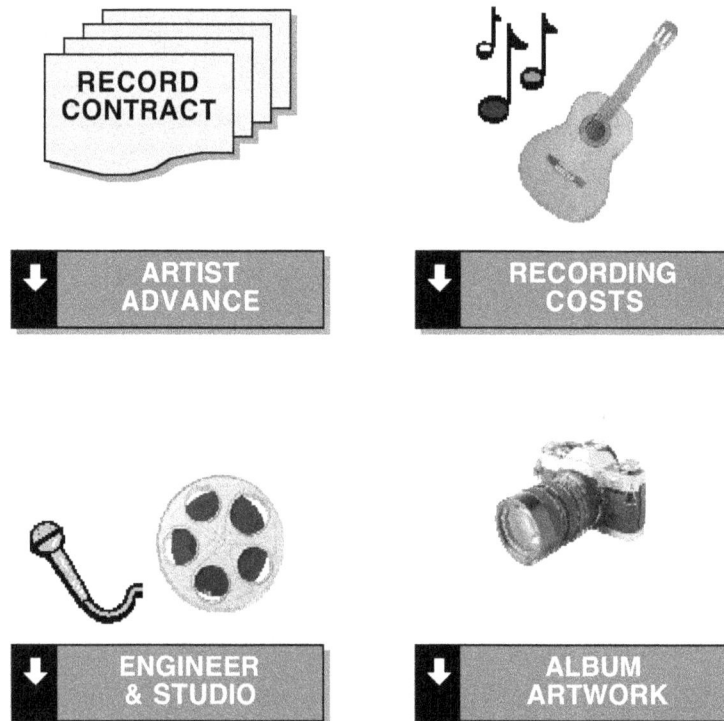

After calculating out the *Gross Artist Royalty Before Recoupment* from sales, recoupable expenses must be repaid before the artist gets a check for royalties. Recoupable costs are defined in the record contract, but usually include all recording costs, the advance, engineers, studio fees, and artwork.

Producers create detailed recording budgets for each record project. An artist that keeps his recording costs low recoups faster.

Recoupable Expenses

RECORD CONTRACT

↓ ARTIST ADVANCE

↓ RECORDING COSTS

↓ ENGINEER & STUDIO

↓ ALBUM ARTWORK

Am I Recouped Yet?

This is the basic question of all recording artists. This section follows the income from the sales of a top–line CD at full SRLP in a normal retail channel.

The customer goes to the store and buys a CD for the SRLP of $12 dollars. The retailer books the sale and keeps $6.00. The remaining $6.00 goes to the record distributor who has the exclusive rights to CD distribution for that territory. The distributor usually keeps $1.00 per unit and remits the rest of the money to the record label. In this example, the label receives $5.00 per CD sold.

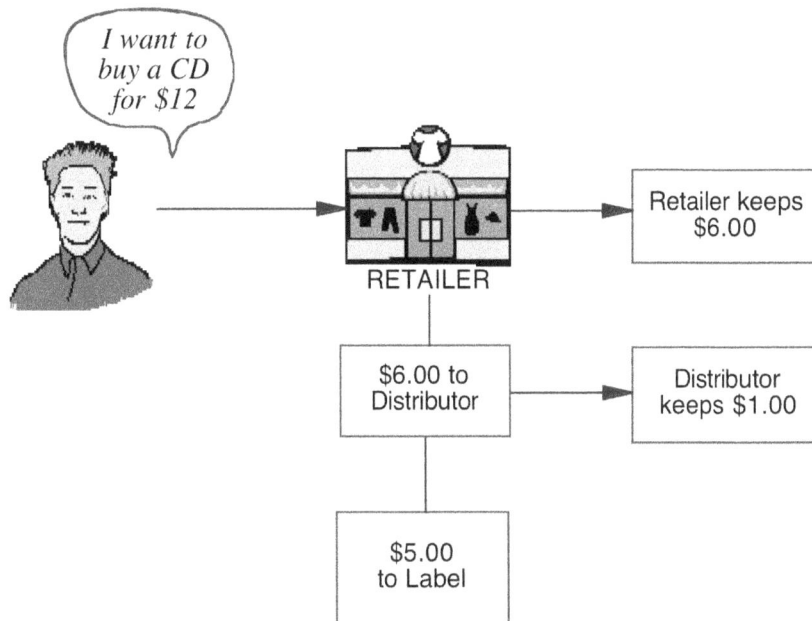

From the proceeds of the sale, the label must pay all §115 mechanical license fees to the publishers. The publishers then split the license income with their writers according to the publishing contract. The label pays all pressing and distribution costs, warehousing, salaries, and overhead from its share, not the artist's. In addition, the label must pay the artist his share of the sales. The *Magic Formula* determines the gross dollar amount of royalties due to the artist before recoupment.

```
                              ┌──────────────────┐
                              │   $ $ $ to Label │
                              └──────────────────┘
                                   │         │
                                   │         │        ┌──────────────────┐
          ┌────────────────────────┘         └───────▶│ §115 Mechanical  │
          ▼                                            │ Licenses         │
┌─────────────────────────┐                            └──────────────────┘
│   ARTIST ROYALTY        │
│   CALCULATION           │                            ┌──────────────────┐
│ Royalty Rate * SRLP *   │                            │ Pressing Costs   │
│ Units Sold              │                            │ Overhead         │
└─────────────────────────┘                            │ Distribution costs│
                                                       │ Salaries         │
                                                       │ Profit           │
                                                       └──────────────────┘
```

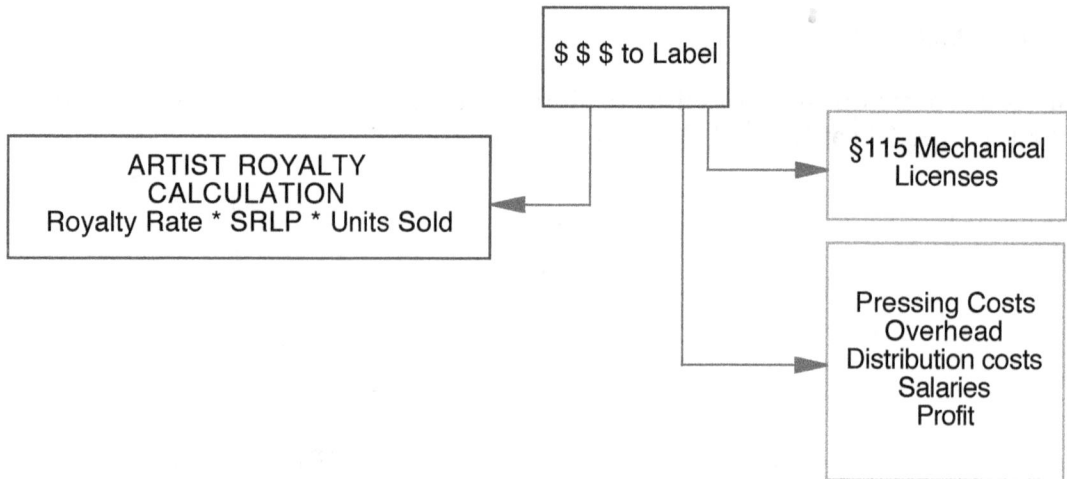

Although there has been a sale, the artist does not see any money from it until he has recouped the advances and recording costs of the album. Advances are pre-paid royalties to the artist. Only after the expenses and packaging deductions are calculated will he get an answer to his question. The artist must also consider the result of *Cross Collateralization* where the artist's royalties from one album are used to recoup against all of artist's other albums.

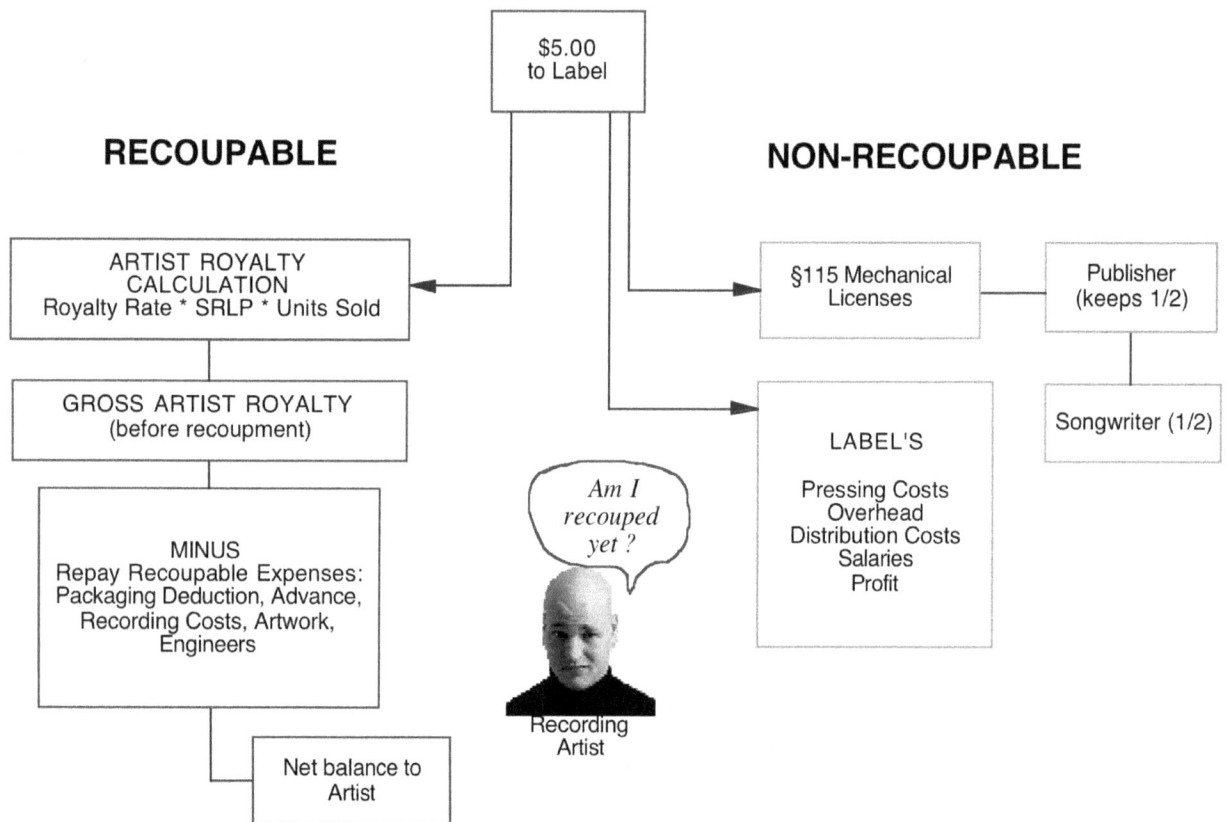

```
                              ┌──────────────────┐
                              │    $5.00         │
                              │    to Label      │
                              └──────────────────┘

   RECOUPABLE                              NON-RECOUPABLE

┌─────────────────────────┐          ┌──────────────┐   ┌──────────────┐
│   ARTIST ROYALTY        │          │ §115         │   │ Publisher    │
│   CALCULATION           │◀─────────│ Mechanical   │───│ (keeps 1/2)  │
│ Royalty Rate * SRLP *   │          │ Licenses     │   └──────────────┘
│ Units Sold              │          └──────────────┘          │
└─────────────────────────┘                                    │
            │                                            ┌──────────────┐
┌─────────────────────────┐                             │ Songwriter   │
│ GROSS ARTIST ROYALTY    │                             │ (1/2)        │
│ (before recoupment)     │                             └──────────────┘
└─────────────────────────┘          ┌──────────────────┐
            │                         │    LABEL'S       │
┌─────────────────────────┐          │                  │
│ MINUS                   │          │ Pressing Costs   │
│ Repay Recoupable        │          │ Overhead         │
│ Expenses:               │          │ Distribution Costs│
│ Packaging Deduction,    │          │ Salaries         │
│ Advance,                │          │ Profit           │
│ Recording Costs,        │          └──────────────────┘
│ Artwork, Engineers      │
└─────────────────────────┘
            │
        ┌──────────────┐
        │ Net balance  │
        │ to Artist    │
        └──────────────┘
```

Am I recouped yet ?

Recording Artist

166

ITUNES

Things can get more complicated with digital audio transmission §106(6) income from iTunes downloads, web streams, satellite broadcasts (Sirius–XM), and other use of the masters in movies or commercials. Frequently the record contract provides that ancillary uses and 3rd party license fees are split equally between the artist and label. The artist's share is still subject to cross-collateralization, and must first go to repay outstanding recoupable expenses.

Apple and labels that distribute their recordings through iTunes do not release how download income is split. The following is an estimate of the cash flow:

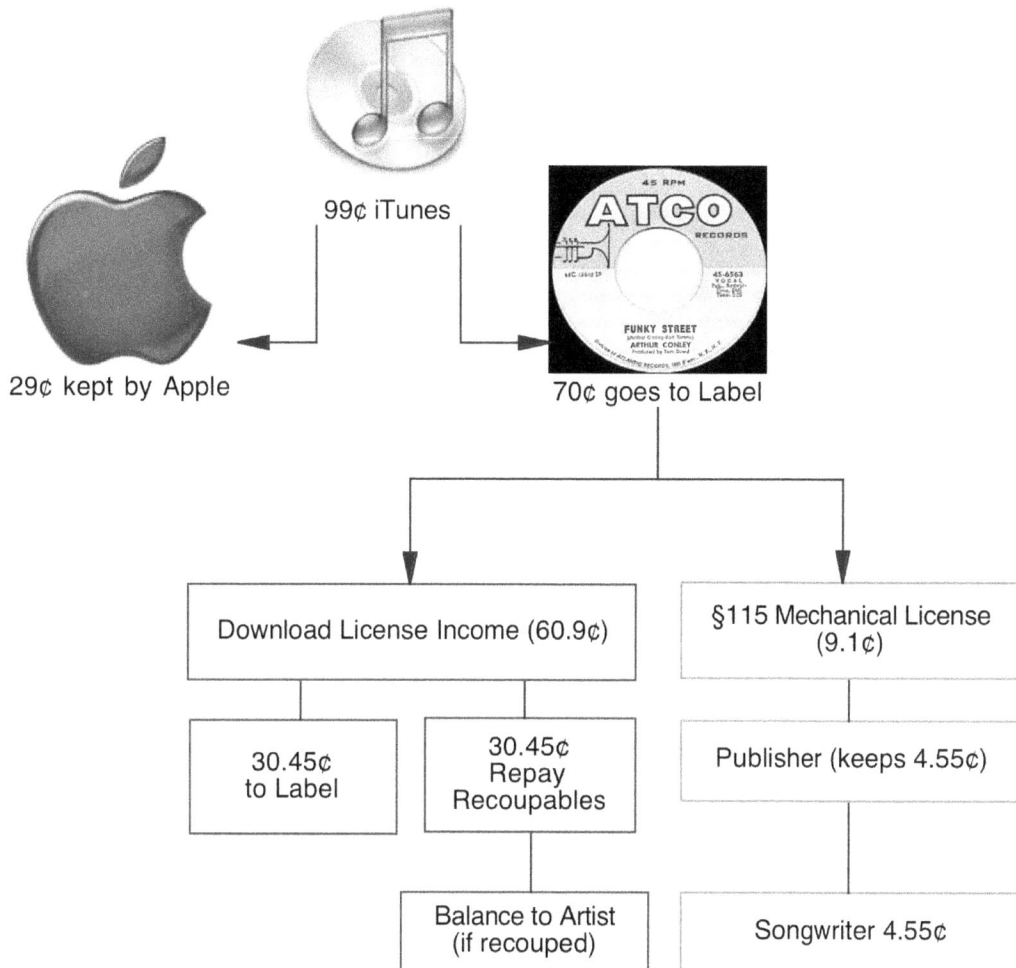

Everyone in the music industry needs a basic understanding of the essential elements of a recording contract and how each element can affect royalties.

APPENDIX A

HANDOUTS

§106 EXCLUSIVE RIGHTS

§106(1) & (3) Make & Sell Copies	§106(4) & (5) Public Performance & Display	§106(2) Derivative Works	§106(6) Digital Audio Transmission (P) only
First Publication	Performing Rights Organizations	Synchronization	Digital Cable
§109 First Sale Doctrine	Foreign PROs	Parody	Internet Streaming
§115 Mechanical License	Grand Rights	Advertising	Satellite Radio
Digital Downloads		Video Games	Podcasts
Sheet Music Folios		Toys	

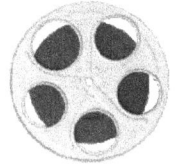

02 THE FOUR ROLES

Songwriter

§106 Exclusive rights in copyrighted works under Form PA ©

    (1) To reproduce the work

    (2) To prepare derivative works

    (3) To distribute & sell copies

    (4) To perform publicly

    (5) To display publicly

    (6) Digital Audio Transmission (for ℗ only)

Duration for new works created after 1/1/78:
        Protection lasts for the life of author + 70 years
        Copyright begins when work is "fixed" by author
        Only author or those claiming rights through author can claim ©

"Work–for–Hire" Employer owns © if:
        Work was created by an employee within scope of employment
or   Work was commissioned by written contract prior to creation

Transfer:
    All © transfers must be in writing, signed by author or owner of rights
    After 35 years, author (or widow & heirs) can terminate assignment of © to others

Registration of Copyright:
    Creates a public record prior to infringement suit
    Prima Facie evidence in court
    If registered w/in 3 months after publication, or before
        infringement, author can sue for damages + attorney fees
    Mechanism to receive compulsory license royalties

Music Publisher

Standard Publishing Agreement:

Songwriter transfers © to Publisher in exchange for the Publisher's promise to pay

a portion of income to the writer.

Publisher protects the work:

Holds the PA © §106 rights by assignment from the songwriter

Sues infringers

Exploits the right to perform and make copies of the song

Authorizes derivatives, translations & arrangements

Income:

Radio, TV, concert, & night club performances

ASCAP, BMI, SESAC (songwriters paid directly)

§115 Mechanical license fees

9.1¢ per copy of the composition

or   1.75¢ per minute (whichever is greater)

Synchronization licenses for movies & TV programs

Advertising and parody uses of the composition

Sales of sheet music copies

Foreign Publishing:

Publishers may license sub-publishers to administer and collect royalties earned by the composition in foreign territories

Co-Publishing:

2 or more publishing companies (one of which is owned by a composer) share in the copyright to the work and the composer gets a larger percentage of the income

Publishing deal:	Co-Publishing deal:
Composer 50¢	Composer 50¢
Publisher 50¢ (100% of ©)	Composer's Publishing Company 25¢ (owns ½ of ©)
	Publisher 25¢ (owns ½ of ©)

Recording Artist

Artists sell their recorded performance to Label for a percentage of record sales

Income from Recording Contract:

    Record Label advances (pre-paid royalties recouped against sales)

    Percentage of album sales after recoupment

Expenses in Recording Contract:

    Repay Label's advance from record royalties

    Repay recoupable expenses from record royalties

Other Income:

    Personal appearances

    Merchandising

    Controlled Composition royalties if Artist is also the Songwriter

Other Expenses:

    Cost of touring

    Fees to Management

    Fees to Booking Agents

MANAGER

    advises Artist on career development

BOOKING AGENT

    obtains dates for live performances

MERCHANDISING COMPANY

    exploits the Artist's name & likeness on T-shirts etc.

PRODUCER

    oversees the recording process at the studio

Record Label

Creates & sells sound recordings of performances by Artist

Owns "Work–for–Hire" sound recording copyright Form SR Ⓟ

    for 95 years from publication or 120 years from creation (whichever is shorter)

Presses CDs

Distributes & sells phonorecords in all formats

Re-mixes the sound recording

Licenses master tapes to TV & movie producers

3 Sources of Income:

    Album sales & digital downloads

    Master Use licenses

        compilations

        sync licenses for TV, movies, advertising

    Digital Audio Transmission §106.6

Expenses:

    Recoupable from Artist's percentage of record sales

        Advances (pre-paid royalties) to Artist

        Recording costs, equipment rental, tape

        Studio & musicians engineering & mixing

        Album artwork

        Independent promotion if allowed by contract

    Non Recoupable (paid by Label)

        Pressing, warehouse & distribution costs

        §115 Mechanical royalties paid to publishers

        Independent promotion if not allowed by contract

        Office expenses & salaries

03 ASSIGNMENT OF COPYRIGHT

KNOW ALL MEN BY THESE PRESENTS, the undersigned copyright owner:

Name: _____

Address: _____

Telephone: _____

SS # : _____

d/o/b: _____

for and in consideration of the sum of $_____ ($____.00) and other valuable consideration, receipt of which is hereby acknowledged, does hereby assign, transfer and set over to the assignee,

      Name: The Big Publishing Company

      Address: 1234 Main St. Big Town, ST

      Tax ID # : 00-0000000

description : _____

_____

_____

_____

created and authored by Assignor together with any and all Assignor's existing copyrights therein throughout the United States and the world, and any and all Assignor's rights of every kind, nature or description attaching to or which may attach to said work and/or embraced by or included in the copyright and any renewal and/or extension thereof, and any actions that may accrue from the date of creation thereof; in the United States and the world.

(If applicable) Which said work the Assignor registered with the Copyright Office of the United States of America on _____, 20___ under Copyright Form _____, Copyright Number _____.

IN WITNESS WHEREOF, the undersigned has executed the foregoing instrument on this _____ day of _____ 20__.

_____   _____
ASSIGNOR   ASSIGNEE
Songwriter   The Big Publishing Company

04 Work–for–Hire Contract

Between   Record Label (Employer)

and   Musician (Employee)

This document confirms that a copyrightable work of intellectual property authorized by Record Label ("Employer") is a "work–for–hire" as specified under §101 of the 1976 Copyright Act of the United States.

Description of the authorized work–for–hire :

_____

_____

It is expressly understood by _____ ("Employee") that his efforts are specially ordered and commissioned, that copyright in the commissioned work shall remain the property of Employer, that all copyright forms will list Employer as an author of a "work made for hire", and that Employer has the sole and exclusive use of the commissioned work and any derivative works made from the commissioned work.

It is further understood that all materials, data, property, recordings, and other items used in the creation of this commissioned work remain the property of Employer, and that Employer retains all rights in these materials, and that Musician may use these materials only for the creation of the commissioned work for hire.

Any unauthorized copying or other use of these materials or the commissioned work by anyone other than Musician for this specific commission will be considered an infringement of Employer's copyright.

In the event that the commissioned work is not considered a "work–for–hire", then it shall be deemed that Musician has assigned to Employer any and all existing copyrights therein throughout the United States and the world, and any and all rights of every kind, nature or description attaching to or which may attach to said work and/or embraced by or included in the copyright and any renewal and/or extension thereof, and any actions that may accrue from the date of creation thereof; in the United States and the world.

Thus done and signed this _____ day of _____, 20___.

_____   _____
Record Label (Employer)   Musician (Employee)
Address   Address
City, State Zip   Telephone (   )
(000) 000-0000   Social Security #
                                     Date of Birth

05 JOINT AUTHOR AGREEMENT

The parties listed below desire to collaborate in the creation of a musical composition entitled _NUTS TO SOUP_.

The parties undertake to create the composition jointly. It is their intention that their individual contributions merge into inseparable or interdependent parts of a unitary whole. The copyright in the composition shall be secured and held jointly by the co-authors in the percentages listed below. All income, licensing fees, and royalties from the composition, as well as from any and all subsidiary rights of every kind, shall be divided as follows:

To	Moe Howard	Fifty percent	(50%)
To	Larry Fine	Forty percent	(40%)
To	Curly Howard	Ten percent	(10%)

Each party shall keep the others fully informed of the progress of all negotiations had in connection with licensing negotiations, or the disposition of any subsidiary rights therein. No license for the use or publication of the composition, or for the disposition of any subsidiary rights therein, shall be valid without the approval of all joint authors/owners.

All moneys shall be paid directly to the joint authors/owners at their respective addresses herein stated.

In all credits, advertisements, posters, or other printed matter used in connection with the composition, the names of the parties shall be listed as joint authors. In no event shall any name appear without the others.

All expenses, which may reasonably be incurred under this agreement, shall be mutually agreed upon in advance, and shall be shared according to the percentage of interest of the parties.

Nothing contained herein creates a partnership between the co-authors. Their relation shall be one of collaboration on a single composition.

The term of this agreement shall be the life of the copyright in the composition and any renewals thereof.

After the death of a joint author, the survivor(s) shall cause to be paid to the estate of the decedent the decedent's share of the proceeds of the composition and of subsidiary rights therein, and furnish to the deceased co-authors' estate a true copy of all agreements pertaining thereto.

This agreement shall be to the benefit of, and shall be binding upon the heirs, executors, administrators, and assigns of the parties.

Agreed this _____ day of _____ 20___, Anytown, ST

Moe Howard
1236 Main Street
Tiny Town, LA 00000
SS #: 111-11-1111
d/o/b: Jan. 1, 1970

Larry Fine
1234 Main Street
Tiny Town, LA 00000
SS #: 222-22-2222
d/o/b: March 5, 1971

Curly Howard
1236 Main Street
Tiny Town, LA 00000
SS #: 333-33-3333
d/o/b: Sept. 18, 1972

06 MECHANICAL LICENSE

Agreement made and entered into on _____ , 20 _____ ,

by and between _____(hereinafter referred to as the "*Publisher*") and

_____ (hereinafter referred to as the "*Label*" or "*Licensee*").

Publisher owns the copyright or controls the exclusive rights to reproduce in Phonorecords and to distribute Phonorecords of the listed copyrighted musical composition.

Licensee has advised the Publisher that it wishes to use said copyrighted work under the compulsory license provision of the Copyright Act (17 U.S. Code §115) relating to the making and distribution of Phonorecords of such work.

Under the following terms and conditions Publisher hereby grants to Label the right to record, reproduce, market and sell the musical composition now entitled:

```
        COMPOSITION :
           WRITER(S) :              %
        PUBLISHER (S) :             %
      ADMINISTRATION :

              ARTIST :
               ALBUM :
              TIMING :

     RECORD COMPANY :
       PHONORECORD # :
        RELEASE DATE :

              FORMAT :
                CD # :
          CASSETTE # :
             VINYL # :
      OTHER FORMAT # :
```

1. Publisher warrants and represents that it is the sole and exclusive proprietor of a valid copyright or license in the listed musical composition, and that Publisher has the right to grant the license herein contained.

2. Publisher grants to Licensee the non-exclusive right, privilege and license, in the United States, during the term of the copyright of said Composition and all renewals and extensions thereof, to use the Composition, and to make and/or use arrangements thereof, in the manufacture and sale of physical "Phonorecords" containing copies of the Composition.

2.a   Upon issue of this license, Licensee shall have all the rights which are granted to, and all the obligations which are imposed upon, users of said copyrighted work under the compulsory license provision of the Copyright Act §115, except that with respect to Phonorecords thereof made and distributed by Licensee.

2.b   The term "Phonorecords," as used herein, means methods of mechanically reproducing the musical Composition limited to, phonograph records, cassette tapes, digital audio tapes, and compact discs.

2.c   This license ***does not*** grant the right to reproduce the Composition by Licensee for the purpose of streaming audio, digital downloads in MP3, or any other computer readable format.

3. Licensee shall pay royalties and account to the Publisher quarterly, within 45 days after the end of each calendar quarter, on the basis of Phonorecords made and distributed.

4. For such Phonorecords made and distributed, the royalty shall be the full statutory rate in effect at the time the Phonorecord is made.

5. This compulsory license covers and is limited to one particular recording of said copyrighted work set forth above as performed by the artist and on the Phonorecord number(s) and in the format(s) set forth above; and this compulsory license does not supersede nor in any way affect any prior agreements now in effect respect to Phonorecords of said copyrighted work.

6. If Licensee fails to account to Publisher and pay royalties as herein provided, Publisher may give written notice that, unless the default is remedied within 30 days from the date of the notice, this compulsory license will be automatically terminated. Such termination shall render either the making and/or the distribution of all Phonorecords for which royalties have not been paid, actionable as acts of intentional infringement under, and fully subject to the remedies provided by the Copyright Act.

7. Licensee needs not serve or file the Notice of Intention to obtain a compulsory license required by the Copyright Act.

8. Publisher hereby indemnifies, and shall hold harmless, Licensee from loss or damage arising out of or connected with any claim by a third party or parties which is inconsistent with any of Publisher's warranties in paragraph 1.

9. This contract is assignable by either party as long as the royalty rate herein stated is paid to Publisher and shall be binding upon the heirs, legal representatives, successors and assigns of the parties hereto.

AGREED TO and entered into by the parties hereto _____ 20 _____

_____   _____
Publisher (© Owner)   Record Label (Licensee)

07 MECHANICAL LICENSE REQUEST

hfa The Harry Fox Agency, Inc., 601 West 26th Street, 5th Floor, New York, NY 10001

Mechanical License Request
(*First Time Licensees Need to Complete New Account Form*)

HFA USE ONLY

Anticipated Quantity of Units ___ Over 2500 ___ 2500 or Under
Failure to check one will delay processing

TRX#_____

Record Company/Licensee Name
_____

Date
_____ / _____ / _____

Address
_____

Contact Name _____ **Fax** _____

City _____ **State** _____ **Zip** _____ **Telephone** _____

Title (One Per Form): _____

Writers: _____

Publisher(s) *(one per line)*	Percentage
_____	%
_____	%
_____	%
_____	%
_____	%

For Manufactures of Over 2500 Units

Song #

M				

Catalog Number-Album

CD_____ Cass_____ Midi_____ LP_____ Digital Comp Cass_____

Minidisk_____ MiniCass_____ DAT_____

Catalog Number-Single

CD single_____ Cassingle_____ Minidisk_____ 12" Single_____ Midi_____

DAT_____ MaxiCass_____ MiniCass_____ 17" Single _____

Rate: Statutory __ Other _____ **Label:** _____

Playing Time **Release Date** **UPC**
_____ / _____ / _____

Artist **ISRC**
_____

Album Title
_____

Explanation
_____

Publishers Approval _____

****PLEASE BE SURE TO COMPLETE ALL APPLICABLE FIELDS****

08 Publishing Contract

AGREEMENT made _____ 20_____ between ZZZ PUBLISHING CO. - BMI (hereinafter called the "Publisher") and ALPHONSE and GASTON jointly (hereinafter called "Writers"):

1. The Writers hereby sell and deliver to the Publisher, a certain heretofore unpublished original musical composition, composed by the above named Writers, now entitled **I LOVE YOU** including the title, words and music, and all copyrights thereof, and all rights, including the grand rights, for the full length of copyright protection.

2. The Writers hereby guaranty that the said composition is their sole, exclusive and original work, and that they have full right and power to make this agreement.

3. The Writers hereby guaranty that the foregoing musical composition does not infringe any other copyrighted work and has been created by the joint collaboration of all the undersigned Writers and not by any independent or separable activity by any of the Writers.

4. In consideration of this agreement, the Publisher agrees to pay the Writers royalties as listed below on the dates and for the accounting periods therein specified:

(a) Ten cents (10¢) per copy with respect to regular piano sheet music copies separately sold and paid for in the United States.

(b) 50% of all net sums actually received by Publisher from mechanical licenses, motion picture, and television synchronization rights and all other rights in the United States.

(c) 50% of all net sums actually received by Publisher from sales and uses in countries outside the United States. It is understood that in such outside countries publication may be made by a Sub-Publisher.

(d) Writers shall not be entitled to share in any sums distributed to Publisher by any performing-rights organization which makes a direct royalty payment to writers.

(e) The Publisher agrees that it will send statements and royalty payments to the Writers within 45 days after June 30th and December 31st of each year.

5. It is understood and agreed by and between all the parties hereto that all sums hereunder payable jointly to the Writers shall be paid to and divided among them respectively as follows:

Writer's Name	Share
ALPHONSE	FIFTY PERCENT (50%)
GASTON	FIFTY PERCENT (50%)

6. If within one year from the date of this contract, Publisher has not performed at least one of the following acts:

(a) published and offered the musical composition for sale in sheet music copies; or

(b) licensed a commercial phonograph record embodying the musical composition to be made; or

(c) licensed the use of the musical composition or any part thereof in or as part of a motion picture, or television picture, or live production, or dramatic or musical production; or

(d) paid to the Writers the sum of Fifty ($50.00) Dollars as an advance against all royalties hereunder.

Then, all rights in and to the musical composition shall automatically revert to the Writers without any further liability on the part of Publisher.

7. The Writers hereby consent to such derivatives, changes, adaptations, translations, dramatizations, editing and arrangements of said composition, and the setting of words to the music and of music to the words, and the change of title as the Publisher deems desirable.

8. Legal action against any alleged infringer of said composition shall be initiated by the Publisher. After deduction of the expense of the litigation, fifty per cent of any recovery shall be paid to the Writer(s).

9. "Writer" as used herein shall be deemed to include all authors and composers signing this agreement.

10. The Publisher shall have the right to assign or license any of its rights and obligations in whole or in part under this agreement to any Sub-Publisher, but that shall not affect the right of the Writer(s) to receive the royalties agreed to from the assignee.

_____
ZZZ PUBLISHING CO. - BMI

Alphonse
_____
Writer: ALPHONSE
1234 Main Street, Town, ST 99999
Soc. Sec. #: 000-00-0000
Year of Birth: 1985

Gaston
_____
Writer: GASTON
4321 Main Street, Town, ST 99999
Soc. Sec. #: 000-00-0000
Year of Birth: 1985

09 RECORDING CONTRACT

1. PARTIES, TERRITORY, TERM

Agreement made as of the _____ day of _____, 20___, by and between, <u>Gigantic Records, Inc.</u> (hereinafter referred to as "Label", "We" or "Us");

and: <u>Larry Fine, Moe Howard, and Curley Howard</u> individually, and collectively performing as the musical group "<u>The Three Stooges</u>" (hereinafter referred to as "Artist" or "You"). Label hereby employs Artist to render exclusive personal services for Label for the purpose of making work-for-hire sound recordings for sale for the territory of the universe.

Term   The term of this agreement will commence on the date hereof and continue, unless extended as provided herein, for a first Contract Period (referred to as the "initial contract period") ending <u>EIGHTEEN (18)</u> months after the date of the commencement of said period.

2. RECORDING PROCEDURE

Recordings will be made pursuant to this agreement in studios as Label may designate. A sufficient number of Performances of Musical Compositions shall be recorded during the initial contract period and each subsequent option period(s) to enable us to produce master recordings (the "Master Recordings" or "Masters") from which can be manufactured a phonorecord consisting of a minimum of <u>Twelve Performances</u> at <u>Sixty (60)</u> minutes playing time (the "Album"). It is understood that the term "Album" may also apply to vinyl phonograph records, cassette tapes, compact discs, audio-visual devices, or other such items now known or hereafter developed which embody selections from the Master Recordings. The Musical Compositions to be recorded shall be agreed to in advance by Label. Artist agrees to work within a recording schedule approved by Label in advance of commencement of recording. Label shall pay all Recording Costs included in said budget as they are incurred.

2a Delivery   Each Master Recording shall be subject to our approval as satisfactory for manufacture and sale.

The Master Recordings shall be fully technically and commercially acceptable, and be edited, sequenced tape from which copies and other transfers can be made for purposes of manufacture along with all paperwork, clearances, and publishing information on all Musical Compositions recorded.

2b Sampling   Further, Artist shall not "sample" any copyrighted composition for use in any Musical Composition recorded hereunder without first obtaining the consent of the owners of the copyrights in the "sampled" works.

3. ROYALTIES

For the rights granted and for the services of Artist in making sound recording works-for-hire, Label shall pay Artist an Advance Royalty of <u>FIFTY THOUSAND DOLLARS ($ 50,000)</u>.

3a Sales Royalties   After Label has recouped all Recording Costs and/or Advanced Royalties paid to Artist relative to the Masters recorded hereunder, Label shall pay Artist a recording royalty of TWELVE PERCENT (12%) (U.S. Base Royalty Rate) of the Suggested Retail List Price ("SRLP") per record for each Record Sold at full SRLP ("Top-Line") in the United States and not returned.

The U.S. Base Royalty Rate will be reduced proportionately for Mid-Line and Budget-Line releases.

3b Producer's Royalty   Royalties paid to Artist are inclusive of the producer's royalty, which shall be paid by Artist.

3c Option Period Royalties   For the first option period, Label shall pay Artist a recording royalty of THIRTEEN PERCENT (13%) of the SRLP per record for each Top-Line record in the United States and not returned under the same terms and conditions.

For the second option period, and all subsequent option periods, Label shall pay Artist a recording royalty of THIRTEEN AND A HALF PERCENT (13.5%) of the SRLP per record for each Top-Line record sold in the United States and not returned under the same terms and conditions.

3d Increase on Sales   The U.S. Base Royalty Rate listed herein shall apply to the first Five Hundred Thousand (500,000) units of net United States sales of each Album released under this contract. For sales in excess of 500,000 units, Label shall increase the applicable U.S. Base Royalty Rate an additional one-half percent (0.5%). For sales in excess of 1,000,000 units, Label shall increase the applicable U.S. Base Royalty Rate an additional one-half percent (0.5%).

3e Foreign Royalties   Label shall pay you as to such other Albums sold outside the United States of America a royalty of one-half the U.S. Base Royalty Rate for the respective numbers of records sold which are not returned, subject to recoupment by Label as outlined above.

3f Compilation and Joint Recordings   In the event that any of the Master Recordings are commercially released with other recordings, it is agreed that as to such a record Artist shall receive that proportion of the royalties payable to you as provided herein before as the number of Master Recordings included in such a record bears to the total number of recordings included in such a record.

In the event that you accompany other royalty artists we shall pay you a royalty proportional to the number of royalty artists and to the contributions of yourself and such other royalty artists as we shall determine and proportional to the royalties otherwise payable to you as provided in this paragraph.

4. ROYALTY ACCOUNTING

Payment of accrued royalties and statement of expenses shall be made semi-annually. Royalty statements shall cover January-June and July-December periods, and shall be rendered within ninety (90) days after each respective half-year period. If any amounts are due, a royalty check shall accompany the statement.

Artist or an authorized representative shall have full right to inspect the relevant books and records of Label or any subsidiaries to ensure that royalties have been properly calculated and paid, provided that reasonable notice is given for such inspection.

4a Recoupable Expenses   We have the right to deduct from the amount of royalties due Artist, any Recording Costs, Advance Royalties previously paid, and any other moneys owed by you to us.

No royalty payments shall be made if Artist's royalty account is unrecouped. If Label owes less than One Hundred Dollars in Artist royalties, said amounts shall be carried over to the next accounting period.

Unless specific objections in writing stating the basis thereof, is given to us within one year from the date of the statement, it shall be agreed that the statement and accounting is complete and accurate and not subject to later objection by Artist.

4b Reserves and Returns   With respect to the computation of royalties, "Records Sold" shall be defined as 100% of records pressed for sale and for which we received payment, less current inventory and returns. Label shall be permitted to keep as a reserve against royalties twenty percent (20%) of income from sales. Reserves will be liquidated over four accounting periods.

4c Cross-Collateralization   Label reserves the right to recoup Advance Royalties from any Album recorded under this contract to "cross-collateralize" against unrecouped Artist's royalty accounts.

If Label begins to pay Artist royalty payments as set forth above and Label later incurs additional Recording Costs and/or pays additional Advance Royalties so that Label goes back to an unrecouped position, Label shall suspend payment of Artist royalties until such time as Label recoups such additional Recording Costs and/or Advance Royalties. Label shall not be obligated to pay Artist a royalty at any time in which Label has not recouped all Recording Costs and/or Advance Royalties from the income earned and received from the sale or licensing of records from any and all sources.

4d Cut-outs and Free Goods   Royalties shall not be payable for promotional records or records given away to induce sales of the Album ("Free Goods"), or sold at less than one-half of the wholesale price ("Cut-outs"). Label will not distribute more than 15% of units pressed as promotional non-royalty bearing Free Goods.

4e Packaging Deductions Label reserves the right to deduct Packaging Charges as recoupable against artist's royalties.

5. EXCLUSIVITY and RE-RECORDING RESTRICTION

Pursuant to this agreement, Artist will not perform as a group, or any member individually, for the purpose of making Sound Recordings of any of the compositions included in the Master Recordings and/or included in the Album(s), for anyone other than Label, without our express contractual permission. This restriction shall apply during the term of this agreement, and for a period of five (5) years after release of the Album which embodies such selections. You hereby acknowledge that your services are unique and extraordinary.

6. COPYRIGHTS

The Master Recordings made under this contract shall from their creation be entirely the property of Label in perpetuity throughout the world, free from of any claim by Artist. Label shall have the right to register its copyright in said sound recordings in Label's name as owner and author of a "work-for-hire" for the full term of copyright. If the sound recordings made under this contract are not considered "works–for–hire", then Artist hereby assigns to Label all of Artist's right, title and interest to the copyright in and to the Master Recordings.

7. MARKETING

Label has the exclusive right to make phonorecords of the performances embodied in the Master Recordings by any method now or hereafter known, and to sell as many copies of the Albums produced under this agreement as possible at whatever price Label deems proper, for as long as desired, under any trademark Label chooses.

7a Release   Label is not under any obligation to release any Master Recordings or Albums recorded under this contract for sale to the public.

7b Name and Likeness   Label has the right to use or to allow others to use Artist's name, likeness, and biographical material for advertising and marketing the Master Recordings and Albums recorded hereunder.

8. WARRANTIES

Artist warrants and represents that no disability or restriction impedes its ability to execute this agreement and perform its terms and conditions. Artist agrees to indemnify and hold Label harmless from any and all loss and damage arising out of or connected with any claim by a third party which is inconsistent with any of the warranties or representations made by Artist in this agreement.

9. MECHANICAL LICENSES

9a Controlled Compositions   You agree that mechanical licenses of any original Musical Compositions written, owned, or composed by you will be licensed to Label at a rate not to exceed seventy five percent (75%) of the then-prevailing "short song formula" statutory rate.

9b Statutory Rate Limit   In order to control its maximum liability for songwriter royalties, it is agreed that Artist shall consult with Label to ensure that final selection of Musical Compositions included in the album shall not result in a liability in excess of ten (10) times the statutory rate. Any mechanical royalty liability in excess of this amount shall be compensated for by Artist, either by payment to Label or by reduction of royalties due Artist.

10. LEASE OF MASTER RECORDINGS

If any Master Recordings produced under this agreement are leased for sale by another company, your artist royalty account will be credited with Fifty Percent (50%) of all payments received by us less expenses incurred by us such as supplying tape copies or metal parts for production of records or jackets to the other company.

11. RENEWAL OPTIONS

You grant Label <u>FIVE (5)</u> options to extend the term for additional Contract Periods ("Option Periods"), under the same terms and conditions applicable to the initial contract period. Each option period shall be for a period of not less than twelve (12) months. Each Album recorded pursuant to any option period must be recorded within six (6) months of the beginning of said option period.

12. ASSIGNMENT

Label may at Label's sole election assign this agreement or any of our rights hereunder to any parent affiliate, subsidiary corporation, or any corporation, partnership, limited liability company, joint venture or firm. Artist may not assign this agreement without the express written approval of Label.

13. SUSPENSION

If Artist is unable, refuses or fails to fulfill the recording commitment, then Label may suspend its obligation hereunder for a number of days between the date of notice of suspension and the date on which Artist actually fulfills Artist's recording commitment.

Artist's services are unique and extraordinary, and the loss thereof cannot be adequately compensated in damages, and Label shall be entitled to injunctive relief to enforce the provisions of this agreement and if such relief is sought, no bond shall be required.

14. DEFINITIONS

Advance Royalty	Prepayment of royalties which must be recouped from royalties earned by Artist from the sale of Albums
Album	A sufficient number of Master Recordings embodying Artist's Performance to comprise a compact disc of not less than 60 minutes of playing time and containing at least twelve different Musical Compositions
Budget-Line Record	Album marketed at 67% or less than Top-Line SRLP
Cut-outs	Albums sold at less than one-half of the wholesale price
Free Goods	Promotional records or records given away to induce sales of the Album
Master Recording	Every recording of sound by any method which is used in the production or manufacture of Albums
Mid-Line Record	Album marketed at 68% to 85% of Top-Line SRLP
Musical Composition	A single musical composition, including all spoken words and bridging passages
Packaging Charges	Reduction in the Artist's royalty in the following percentages:

	Compact Discs	25%
	Cassettes	15%
	Vinyl	15%
	All other media	15%

Performance	Singing, speaking, conducting or playing an instrument, alone or with others

Recording Costs	All payments made by Label which are related to the production of the Master Recordings, including without limitation, travel, rehearsal, equipment rental, cartage, transportation costs, hotel, living expenses, studio costs, engineers, tape, side musicians, mastering, mixing, Album artwork, photography, graphic design, packaging, payments to third parties, and any moneys advanced to Artist.
Records Sold	100% of records pressed for sale and for which Label received payment, minus current inventory and returns
SRLP	Suggested Retail List Price in the United States established by Label or its licensees
Top-Line Record	Album marketed at 100% of SRLP
U.S. Base Royalty Rate	A percentage of Top–Line Suggested Retail List Price less all taxes for albums sold in the U.S. through normal retail channels and not returned.

15. ENTIRE AGREEMENT

This agreement sets forth the entire agreement and understanding between Label and Artist with respect to the subject matter contained herein. No modification, amendment, waiver, termination or discharge of this agreement or any provision hereof shall be binding upon either of you or us unless confirmed by a written instrument signed by Label and Artist.

This agreement shall be deemed to have been made and performed in the State of Louisiana and its validity, construction and effect shall be governed by its laws.

AGREED TO AND ACCEPTED this _____ day of _____ 20____ :

Ebenezer Scrooge
Gigantic Records, Inc. (Label)
P.O. Box 0000
Metropolis, LA 00000

Larry Fine
Artist
1234 Main Street
Tiny Town, LA 00000

Moe Howard
Artist
1236 Main Street
Tiny Town, LA 00000

Curly Howard
Artist
1236 Main Street
Tiny Town, LA 00000

10 RECORDING BUDGET

SAMPLE ESTIMATED RECORDING BUDGET

Artist : _____
Producer : _____
Project : _____

PRE-PRODUCTION

Rehearsal Facility	_____	days @	$	-	per day =	$	-
Programming						$	-
Miscellaneous						$	-
TOTAL PRE-PRODUCTION						$	-

STUDIO

Tracks	_____	days @	$	-	per day =	$	-
	_____	hours @	$	-	per hour =	$	-
Overdubs	_____	days @	$	-	per day =	$	-
	_____	hours @	$	-	per hour =	$	-
Lead Vocals	_____	days @	$	-	per day =	$	-
	_____	hours @	$	-	per hour =	$	-
Background Vocals	_____	days @	$	-	per day =	$	-
Mixing		days @	$	-	per day =	$	-
TOTAL STUDIO						$	-

TAPE

Analog	_____	2" reels @	$	-	each =	$	-
	_____	1/2" reels @	$	-	each =	$	-
	_____	1/4" reels @	$	-	each =	$	-
	_____	cassettes @	$	-	each =	$	-
Digital	_____	2 track reels @	$	-	each =	$	-
	_____	multi track reels @	$	-	each =	$	-
	_____	DATs @	$	-	each =	$	-
		CD-ROMs @	$	-	each =	$	-
TOTAL TAPE						$	-

TALENT

Tracks—Non-royalty Artists	_____	musicians @	$	-	leader scale =	$	-
	_____	musicians @	$	-	single scale =	$	-
	_____	musicians @	$	-	double scale =	$	-
Overdubs—Non-royalty Artists	_____	musicians @	$	-	leader scale =	$	-
	_____	musicians @	$	-	single scale =	$	-
	_____	musicians @	$	-	double scale =	$	-
Royalty Artists	_____	musicians @	$	-	per day =	$	-
Arrangers					flat fee =	$	-
Vocals	_____	tracks	$	-	per track =	$	-
Rhythm	_____	tracks	$	-	per track =	$	-
Copyist	_____	tracks	$	-	per track =	$	-

VOCALS

Royalty Artist (Union Pension & Welfare)						$	-
Guest Artists (Union Pension & Welfare)						$	-
Background Vocals	_____	singers	$	-	per day =	$	-
		singers	$	-	per track =	$	-
TOTAL TALENT & VOCALS						$	-

ENGINEER							
	_____	days @	$	-	per day =	$	-
Tracks	_____	hours @	$	-	per hour =	$	-
Overdubs	_____	days @	$	-	per day =	$	-
Lead Vocals	_____	days @	$	-	per day =	$	-
Background Vocals	_____	days @	$	-	per day =	$	-
Flat Fee						$	-
TOTAL ENGINEER						$	-

EQUIPMENT RENTAL							
Item #1	_____	days @	$	-	per day =	$	-
Item #2	_____	days @	$	-	per day =	$	-
Item #3	_____	days @	$	-	per day =	$	-
Miscellaneous Rental	_____	days @	$	-	per day =	$	-
Mixing outboard	_____	days @	$	-	per day =	$	-
Cartage						$	-
Purchases						$	-
TOTAL EQUIPMENT RENTAL						$	-

TRAVEL & LIVING EXPENSES							
Per Diems	_____	days @	$	-	per day =	$	-
Air Fares	_____	tickets @	$	-	each =	$	-
Rental Cars	_____	days @	$	-	per day =	$	-
Hotel Rooms	_____	days @	$	-	per day =	$	-
TOTAL TRAVEL & LIVING						$	-

MISCELLANEOUS							
General Misc.						$	-
Production Assistant	_____	days @	$	-	per day =	$	-
Ground Transportation	_____	days @	$	-	per day =	$	-
License Fees for Sampling						$	-
TOTAL MISC.						$	-

MASTERING & POST PRODUCTION							
Engineer	_____	hours @	$	-	per hour =	$	-
Reference Masters	_____	masters	$	-	each =	$	-
	_____	DATs @	$	-	each =	$	-
		CD-ROMs @	$	-	each =	$	-
TOTAL MASTERING						$	-

ADVANCES		
Royalty Artist Advance	$	-
Guest Royalty Artist Advance	$	-
Producer's Advance	$	-
TOTAL ADVANCES	$	-

TOTAL ESTIMATED RECORDING BUDGET $ -

Approved by Producer : _____   date   ____ / ____ / ____

Approved by Artist : _____   date   ____ / ____ / ____

Approved by Label : _____   date   ____ / ____ / ____

11 Am I Recouped?

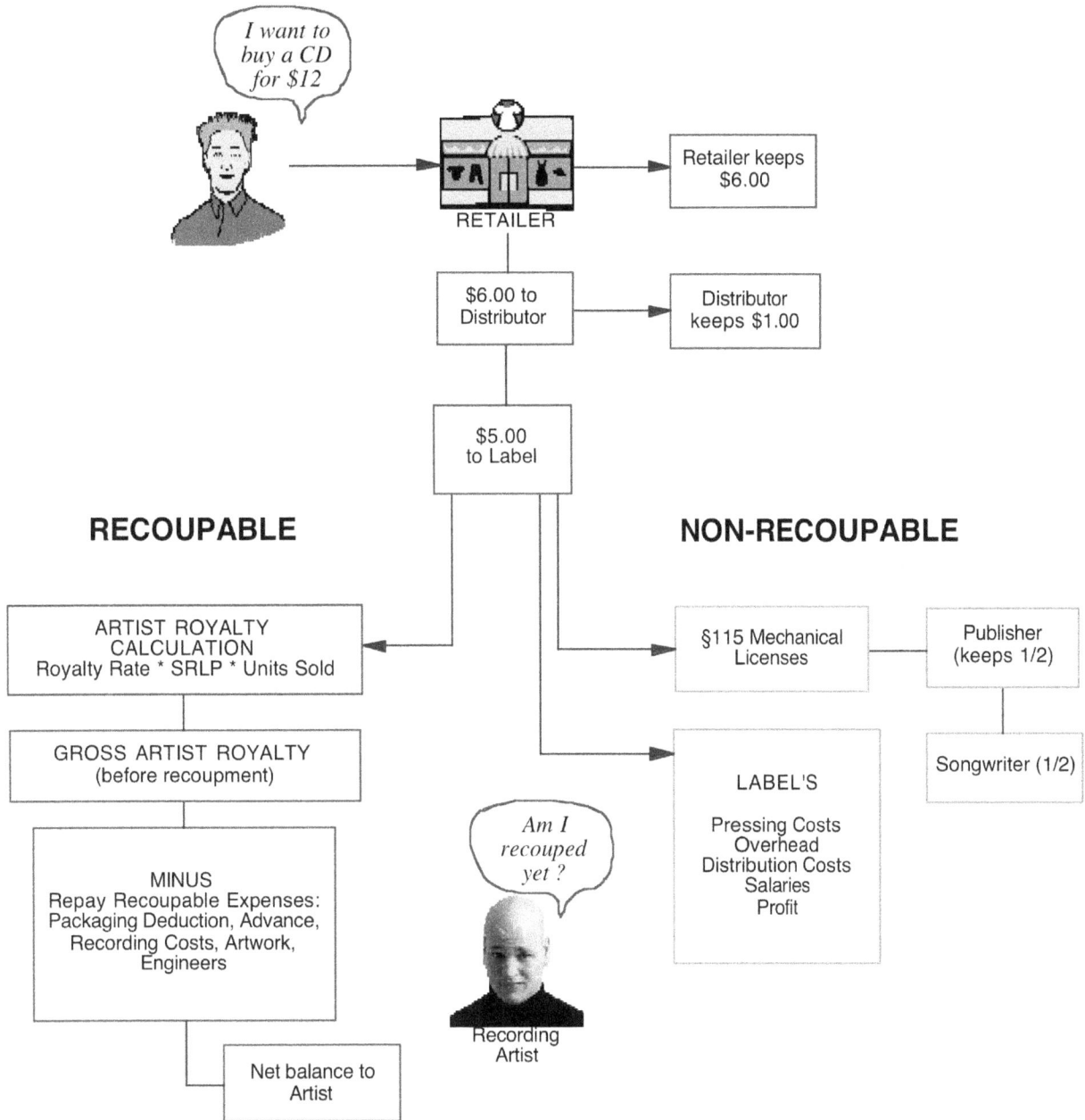

I want to buy a CD for $12

RETAILER

Retailer keeps $6.00

$6.00 to Distributor

Distributor keeps $1.00

$5.00 to Label

RECOUPABLE

NON-RECOUPABLE

ARTIST ROYALTY CALCULATION
Royalty Rate * SRLP * Units Sold

GROSS ARTIST ROYALTY
(before recoupment)

MINUS
Repay Recoupable Expenses:
Packaging Deduction, Advance,
Recording Costs, Artwork,
Engineers

Net balance to Artist

Am I recouped yet ?

Recording Artist

§115 Mechanical Licenses

Publisher (keeps 1/2)

Songwriter (1/2)

LABEL'S

Pressing Costs
Overhead
Distribution Costs
Salaries
Profit

12 ARTIST RECORDING ROYALTY STATEMENT

Sample Artist Royalty Statement
for the period Jan. 1 through June 30

Artist: Oliver Twist
Project: Twist & Shout

Income :	Royalty Rate by format	SRLP by format	Units Sold this period	Gross Artist Royalty
CD Release #1450	12.5%	$14.98	8,154	$15,268.37
Cassette Release #1451	10.5%	$9.98	4,056	$4,250.28
EP Release #1452	10.0%	$5.98	145	$86.71
iTunes (50% of net to Label)	50.0%	$0.61	5,349	$1,628.77
Artist Royalty before recoupment			17,704	$21,234.13
Plus Foreign Royalties				$0.00
Plus License Income				$0.00
Total this period				$21,234.13

Deductions :			
Container Charge: CD	-25.0%		-$3,817.09
Container Charge: CS	-15.0%		-$637.54
Container Charge: EP	-15.0%		-$13.01
Recoupable expenses			
Producer (flat fee)		-2,500.00	
Recording Costs		-25,000.00	
Album artwork & graphics		-750.00	
Artist Advance		-15,000.00	
Total Recoupable		-43,250.00	-$43,250.00
Less reserve against returns	-20.0%		-$4,246.83
Plus liquidation of prior reserves			$0.00
Balance last statement			$0.00

Total due to Artist :   -$30,730.34
(if negative, amount to be recouped)

I hereby certify that the above is a true and accurate accounting of the royalties due at this time
Bob Cratchit   Royalty Dept.
Paid with check #   n/a   Date issued :   Amount :   n/a
* Amounts less than $100 are not paid until accumulated royalties exceed $100.

Sample Artist Royalty Statement
for the period July 1 through Dec. 31

Artist: Oliver Twist
Project: Twist & Shout

Income :	Royalty Rate by format	SRLP by format	Units Sold this period	Gross Artist Royalty
CD Release #1450	12.5%	$14.98	16,199	$30,332.63
Cassette Release #1451	10.5%	$9.98	1,542	$1,615.86
EP Release #1452	10.0%	$5.98	79	$47.24
iTunes (50% of net to Label)	50.0%	$0.61	38,257	$11,649.26
Artist Royalty before recoupment			56,077	$43,644.99
Plus Foreign Royalties				$0.00
Plus License Income (50% of net to Label)				$5,000.00
Total this period				$48,644.99

Deductions :			
Container Charge: CD	-25.0%		-$7,583.16
Container Charge: CS	-15.0%		-$242.38
Container Charge: EP	-15.0%		-$7.09

Recoupable expenses		
Producer (flat fee)	0.00	
Recording Costs	0.00	
Album artwork & graphics	0.00	
Artist Advance	0.00	
Total Recoupable	0.00	$0.00

Less reserve against returns	-20.0%	-$9,729.00
Plus liquidation of prior reserves		$4,246.83
Balance last statement		-$30,730.34

Total due to Artist :   **$4,599.86**
(if negative, amount to be recouped)

I hereby certify that the above is a true and accurate accounting of the royalties due at this time
Bob Cratchit   Royalty Dept.
Paid with check # 301414   Date issued : Feb 15   Amount : $4,599.86
* Amounts less than $100 are not paid until accumulated royalties exceed $100.

APPENDIX B

DISCOGRAPHY

"Washington Post March", (J.P. Sousa) performed by The U.S. Marine Band 1890

"Washington Post March", (J.P. Sousa) performed by The U.S. Marine Band 1989

"Maple Leaf Rag", (S. Joplin) performed by Scott Joplin on piano roll 1916

"Supercalifragilisticexpialidocious", (Richard Sherman, Robert Sherman) from the *Mary Poppins* soundtrack

Symphony No. 9, 4th Movement, (Beethoven) Berliner Philharmoniker, 1984

"Candle in the Wind (Goodbye Norma Jean)" (E. John, B. Taupin) from the album *Goodbye Yellow Brick Road* 1974

"Candle in the Wind 1997 (Goodbye England's Rose)" (E. John, B. Taupin) The single was released world-wide in 1997 and sold over 22 million copies. Sir Elton John performed the song live only once, at the funeral of Princess Diana, September 6, 1997.

"Unforgettable", (I. Gordon) original recording performed by Nat King Cole, Capitol Records 1962

"Unforgettable", (I. Gordon) from the album *Unforgettable With Love*, duet performed by Nat King Cole and Natalie Cole, ℗ Elektra Records 1991. Grammy Awards for Song of the Year, Record of the Year and Best Traditional Pop Vocal Performance 1992

"Every Breath You Take", (Sting) from the album *Synchronicity*, performed by The Police. Grammy Award for Best Pop Performance by a Duo or Group with Vocal 1984

"Every Breath You Take", (Sting) performed by Puff Daddy and Sting at the MTV Video Awards September 4, 1997.

"99 Luftballons", (P.J. Fahrenkrog, C. Karges, & K.J. McAlea), sung in German by Nena

"99 Red Balloons", (P.J. Fahrenkrog, C. Karges, & K.J. McAlea), sung in English by Nena

"99 Red Balloons", (P.J. Fahrenkrog, C. Karges, & K.J. McAlea), performed in English and German by Goldfinger

"The Look of Love", (B. Bacharach, H. David) from the *Casino Royale* soundtrack, performed by Dusty Springfield

"Layla", (E. Clapton, J.B. Gordon), from the album *Layla and Other Assorted Love Songs* performed by Derek and the Dominos 1970

"Layla", (E. Clapton, J.B. Gordon), performed by Eric Clapton MTV Unplugged 1992

"I Will Always Love You", (D. Parton) from the album *Jolene* performed by Dolly Parton 1974

"I Will Always Love You", (D. Parton) from *The Bodyguard: Original Soundtrack Album* performed by Whitney Houston 1992

"My Way", (Anka, Revaux, Thibault) recorded December 30, 1968 by Frank Sinatra

"My Way", (Anka, Revaux, Thibault) performed January 12, 1973 by Elvis Presley

"My Way", (Anka, Revaux, Thibault) performed by Sid Vicious

"The Star Spangled Banner", (F.S. Key) performed January 2000 at from Super Bowl XXXIV by Faith Hill

"The Star Spangled Banner", (F.S. Key) performed on August 17, 1969 at The Woodstock Music and Art Fair by Jimi Hendrix & A Band of Gypsies

"Purple Haze", (Hendrix) from the album *Are You Experienced?* performed by The Jimi Hendrix Experience

"Purple Haze", (Hendrix, arranged by S. Riffkin) from the album *Kronos Quartet*, performed by The Kronos Quartet 1986

"Die Moritat Von Mackie Messer" from *Die Dreigroschenoper* (Weill)

"Mackie Messer", (Brecht, Weill) performed by Hildegard Knef

"Mack The Knife", (Brecht, Weill) instrumental performed by Dick Hyman 1956

"A Theme From The Threepenny Opera (Mack The Knife)", (Blitzstein, Brecht, Weill) Columbia Records performed by Louis Armstrong 1955

"Mack The Knife", (Blitzstein, Brecht, Weill) recorded by Bobby Darin 1958, Grammy Award for Record of the Year 1959

"Light My Fire" (Densmore, Krieger, Manzarek, Morrison) from the album *The Doors*, performed by The Doors 1967

"Light My Fire" (Densmore, Krieger, Manzarek, Morrison) performed by Jose Feliciano, Grammy Award for Best Contemporary Pop Vocal Performance, Male 1968

"Boogie Chillen", (Hooker, Besman) performed by John Lee Hooker

"La Grange", (Beard, Gibbons, Hill) from the album *Tres Hombres* performed by ZZ Top

"He's So Fine", (R. Mack) performed by The Chiffons

"My Sweet Lord", (Harrison) performed by George Harrison

"Super Freak", (J.A. Johnson, [a/k/a Rick James], A. Miller) published by Jobete Music Co., Inc. from the album *Street Scenes*, Motown Record Company 1981

"(U) Can't Touch This", (K. Burrell [a/k/a MC Hammer, J.A. Johnson, [a/k/a Rick James], A. Miller) administered by Jobete Music Co. Inc. for Jobete Music Co., Stone City Music, Stone Diamond Music Corporation, Bust-it Publishing) from the album *Please Hammer don't Hurt 'em*, Capitol Records 1990

Kanon und Gigue in D-Dur, (J. Pachelbel) from the album *Musica Antiqua Koln* conducted by Reinhard Goebel

"Hook", (J. Popper) from the album *Four* performed by Blues Traveler

"Graduation Song (Friends Forever)", (J. Deutsch, C. Fitzpatrick) performed by Vitamin C, MIDI

"Oh, Pretty Woman", (Orbison & Dees) performed by Roy Orbison

"Pretty Woman", (Campbell parody) performed by 2 Live Crew

"Gangsta's Paradise", (Ivey, Rasheed, Sanders, Wonder) performed by Coolio

"Amish Paradise", (Ivey, Rasheed, Sanders, Wonder) performed by "Weird Al" Yankovic

www.ingramcontent.com/pod-product-compliance
Lightning Source LLC
Chambersburg PA
CBHW080544220326
41599CB00032B/6359